# The Good Enough Job

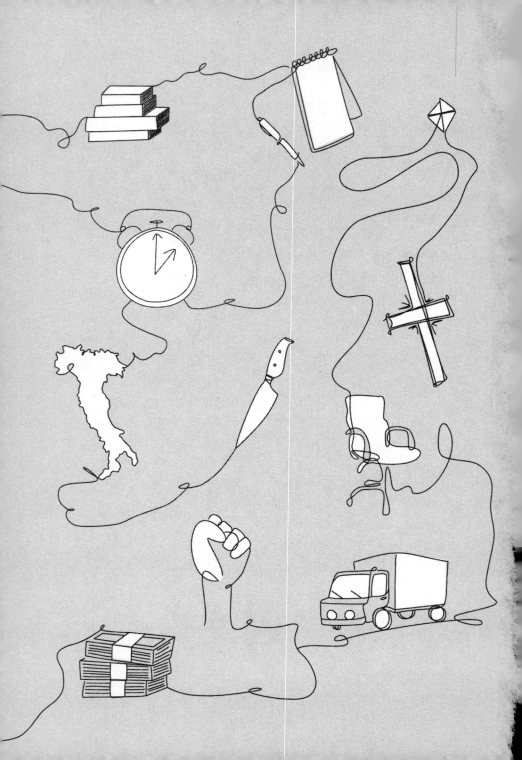

# The Good Enough Job

~ℓ~

## RECLAIMING LIFE FROM WORK

## Simone Stolzoff

PORTFOLIO / PENGUIN

Portfolio / Penguin
An imprint of Penguin Random House LLC
penguinrandomhouse.com

Most Portfolio books are available at a discount when purchased in quantity for sales
promotions or corporate use. Special editions, which include personalized covers, excerpts,
and corporate imprints, can be created when purchased in large quantities. For more
information, please call (212) 572-2232 or e-mail specialmarkets@penguinrandomhouse.com.
Your local bookstore can also assist with discounted bulk purchases using the Penguin
Random House corporate Business-to-Business program. For assistance in locating a
participating retailer, e-mail B2B@penguinrandomhouse.com.

Illustrations by Katy Hill

ISBN 9780593538968 (hardcover)
ISBN 9780593538975 (ebook)

Printed in the United States of America
1st Printing

BOOK DESIGN BY ALISSA ROSE THEODOR

Some names and identifying characteristics have been changed to
protect the privacy of the individuals involved.

*To my parents,*
*for each modeling lives beyond work*

# Contents

*He who knows he has enough is rich.*

LAO-TZU

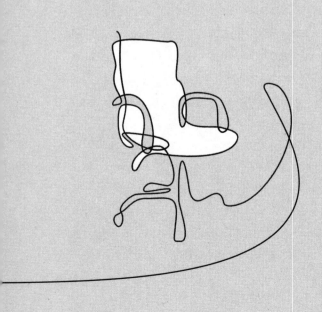

# How Work Became More than a Job

A businessman is sitting on the beach of a small fishing village when he sees a fisherman approach the shore with his daily haul. Impressed by the quality of the fish, the businessman asks the fisherman how long it took him to bring in his catch.

"Oh, just a short while," the fisherman replies.

"Why don't you stay out longer to catch more fish?" the businessman asks.

"Because this is all I need."

"But then what do you do with your time?"

"I sleep late, catch a few fish, play with my kids, take a nap with my wife, and then join my buddies in town to drink wine and play guitar," the fisherman responds.

The businessman is shocked. He explains that he has an MBA,

and that if the fisherman follows his advice, he could help him grow his business. "You could buy a bigger boat," the businessman says, "and then use the proceeds to open your own cannery."

"Then what?" the fisherman asks.

"Then you could move to the city to open a distribution center."

"And then what?"

"Then you could expand your business internationally, and eventually take your company public," the businessman says. "When the time is right, you can sell your shares and become very rich!"

"And then what?"

"Well, then you can retire, move to a small fishing village, sleep late, catch a few fish, play with your kids, take naps with your wife, and join your buddies in town to drink wine and play guitar."

The fisherman smiles at the businessman and continues down the beach.

I love this little parable. It's an adaptation of a German short story from 1963 and has since been translated and shared widely. But there's something particularly American about the businessman's work-centric worldview. The United States' mantra might as well be "I produce, therefore I am."

For Americans, "What do you do?" is often the first question we ask when we meet someone new. I remember once asking a Chilean guy I met at a hostel what he did. "You mean for work?" he responded, as if I had asked for the balance of his bank account. Of course, we do all manner of things. But in the United States, how we make money is shorthand for who we are. Our livelihoods have become our lives.

When analysts from the Pew Research Center asked Americans what gives their life meaning, respondents were nearly two times more likely to name their career than to name their spouse. Work was a greater source of meaning than both faith and friends. Another study found that 95 percent of American teenagers— teenagers!—ranked having a career or job they enjoyed as "extremely or very important to them as an adult." A fulfilling career ranked higher than any other priority, including making money and helping people in need.

And yet the fetishization of work is not unique to the United States. In an increasingly globalized world, busyness knows no borders. American work culture and management systems are cultural exports as much as Big Macs and Levi's jeans. Those of you reading these pages outside of the U.S. know that many of the trends and examples of Americans' relationship to work echo the experience of workers in other countries, too—especially among the highest earners.

For white-collar professionals, jobs have become akin to a religious identity: in addition to a paycheck, they provide meaning, community, and a sense of purpose. Journalist Derek Thompson dubbed this new phenomenon "workism." A workist seeks meaning from their work similar to how a religious person seeks meaning from their faith. According to Thompson, over the course of the twentieth century work has evolved from a chore to a status to a means of self-actualization. A look at my own family history bears out this theory.

My Italian grandmother did not expect work to be a reflection of her identity. After my grandfather passed away, she did what she had to do to take care of their five children. She opened a coffee shop in a small town in the heel of Italy's boot and worked there for thirty years. Until her death, she had a single bulbous bicep from repeatedly pulling down the manual lever of the espresso machine. Her identity was straightforward. First, she was a woman of faith. Then a mother, a grandmother, a sister, a fresh-pasta maker. She enjoyed her work at the coffee shop—loved it, even—but it did not define her.

My mother was raised in the same Italian town where all her siblings still live. If she had followed the prescribed path, she would have gone to the local university, bought a house within walking distance of her childhood home, and joined the rest of the family for orecchiette every day around one. (In her hometown, shops and offices close in the afternoons for *riposo*, a few hours for workers to tend to nonwork priorities like family, food, and rest.)

My mom, however, got a scholarship to study in Rome, met a cute American guy at a holiday party in Switzerland, and moved to San Francisco. She pursued a graduate degree in psychology out of a desire for economic stability as much as out of personal interest. She also loves her work, but very much treats it as a means to an end. She works so she can buy heirloom tomatoes from the farmers' market, fly back to Italy every summer, and invest in her son's education.

My dad is also a psychologist, and probably the closest in my family to a workist. I remember asking him once about the philanthropic cause he cares most about. "I see my work as a type of philanthropy," he told me of his psychology practice. "My work is my way of giving back." My dad wants to work for as long as he can still remember his patients' names. Even during pandemic lockdowns, he returned to the office whenever he could.

My family history points toward some of the central themes of this book: that workism is particularly American, though it certainly exists in other places, too; that workism is especially common among the privileged, though it also exists in communities of less privilege; and finally, that workism is a relatively new phenomenon, more common among my generation than my grandparents'. The modern ideology of workism asks two distinct pursuits—money and inner fulfillment—to coalesce. These pursuits are not always aligned, and yet we increasingly look to our jobs to satisfy both.

But mostly I share a bit of my family history so you can get a sense of who I am. My name is Simone, and I'm a workist. Or at least, a recovering one. Throughout my life, I've wanted to be a journalist, a designer, a lawyer, a diplomat, a poet, and a shortstop for the San Francisco Giants. I've spent my career searching for a vocational soulmate, for a job that doesn't just pay the bills but is a unique reflection of who I am.

However, this book is not a memoir. Though the topic is close to my heart, I wanted to investigate why work has become central to not just mine but so many people's identities. I interviewed more than one hundred workers—from corporate lawyers in Manhattan to kayak guides in Alaska, stay-at-home parents in Copenhagen to fast-food workers in California—to select the nine people profiled in the chapters to come. I chose to focus primarily (but not exclusively) on the stories of white-collar workers in the United States for two reasons.

First, the United States is in the midst of a nationwide trend that defies both history and logic. Throughout history, wealth has been inversely correlated with how many hours people work. The more wealth you have, the less you work because, well, you can afford not to. But in the last half century, the highest earners are responsible for some of the greatest *increases* in work time. That is to say, the same Americans who can afford to work the least are working more than ever.

Second, I chose to focus primarily on white-collar workers because they're the most likely to look to work for meaning and identity. This phenomenon holds true for high earners across the world. From Sweden to South Korea, wealthier and more educated adults mention their job as a source of meaning at about twice the rate of low earners and people without college degrees. Among other reasons, high earners are less likely to have other sources of meaning, like organized religion, in their lives.

But although professional culture treats work as the central axis around which the rest of life orbits, the majority of workers in the world do not work to self-actualize; they work to survive. "People who love what they do, those people are blessed, man," Hamza Taskeem, a cook who has worked in the same Pakistani restaurant for eighteen years, told me. "I just work to get by."

That said, few Americans are immune to the *culture* of workism in this country. Regardless of class, nearly every worker I spoke to commented on the pressure of living in a country where self-worth and work are so tightly bound. Here, capitalism is not just an economic system; it's also a social philosophy—a philosophy that says a person is as valuable as their output. In the United States, productivity is more than a measurement; it's a moral good.

To understand workism in the U.S. today, it helps to look back at how we got here. Two hundred years ago, almost no one had a career—at least not in the way we currently conceive of careers as stories of progress and change. The majority of Americans were farmers, as were their parents and grandparents. A farmer's hours are dictated by the sun, not by a boss or a scheduling algorithm. The intensity of work follows the cycle of the seasons: busy during the harvest, more idle during the winter. However, the industrial revolution ushered us into an era where productivity was no longer limited by seasons and sunlight. By the mid-nineteenth century, factory workers regularly worked ten- or twelve-hour days, six or seven days a week.

Though today "nine-to-five" has become synonymous with the workday, contemporary standards such as the eight-hour day, forty-hour week, and two-day weekend were not always the norm. The organized labor movement fought hard to win them for workers. "Eight hours for work, eight hours for rest, eight hours for what we will" read the signs at the inaugural May Day protests in Chicago in 1886. While conventions around how, when, and why we work have since become standardized, they are neither natural nor fixed. They were negotiated before and can be negotiated again.

A less work-centric society has been a recurring American dream. In his 1930 essay "Economic Possibilities for Our Grand-children," economist John Maynard Keynes famously predicted that by 2030 we would work only fifteen hours a week. Keynes believed one of the most pressing questions of the twenty-first century would be how we'd occupy our leisure. As recently as 1965, Congress held a lengthy hearing to discuss the imminent twenty-hour workweek. Elected officials worried that by the year 2000, Americans would take so many vacations that we would have to overhaul our national infrastructure to accommodate the increase in trips. Alas, visions of five-day weekends and co-pious free time have yet to materialize.

For the majority of the twentieth century, however, pressure from unions and productivity gains from technological advances actually *did* drive down working hours for the average American. But while our developed-world peers continued to reduce their work time, by the end of the century some Americans started working more than ever. In 1975, Americans and Germans worked the exact same number of hours on average. In 2021, Americans worked more than 30 percent more.

There are many possible answers to the question of why Americans work so damn much. There are economic factors. Stagnant wages have forced many workers to work more to buy the same loaf of bread. There are political factors. In the 1950s, one in three working Americans belonged to a union; by 2021, that number had decreased to one in ten, leaving many workers without a collective bargaining apparatus to demand better conditions. And there are ideological factors. Capitalism and a Protestant work ethic were, after all, the two strands that entwined to form our country's DNA.

But over the past several decades, the United States has also undergone a profound cultural shift that amplifies each of the factors above. There is a growing expectation that work ought to be a source of personal fulfillment and meaning. Call it the new American work ethic.

This new ethic changed the relationship millions of people have to their work. Rather than conceptualize their work as labor, working in solidarity with people across different roles, industries, and classes, many white-collar workers began to see their work as a reflection of their individual passions and identities. As sociologist Jamie K. McCallum writes in his book *Worked Over: How Round-the-Clock Work Is Killing the American Dream*, "When work was dirty, less was more; now that it's meaningful, more is better."

The title *The Good Enough Job* is an allusion to "good enough" parenting, a theory devised in the 1950s by the British psychoanalyst and pediatrician Donald Woods Winnicott. Winnicott observed a growing idealization of parenting. The perfect parent did everything in their power to prevent their baby from feeling pain. And if the baby expressed anything negative, the parent took it personally.

Winnicott believed both the parent and the child would benefit from an approach of sufficiency over perfection. The "good enough" parent, as opposed to the perfect parent, offers support but also enough space so that their baby learns to self-soothe. As a result, the baby develops resiliency, and the parent does not become lost in their baby's feelings.

A similar idealization is occurring in the workplace. Hell, I'm writing this sentence from a WeWork where "Always Do What You Love" is plastered on the side of my coffee mug. Given how much we work, it follows that the choice of what to do—at least for those who have the privilege of choice—should be one of the most consequential decisions we make. Why not pursue a career with the same gusto with which we might pursue a life partner?

The answer, in short, is that the expectation that work will always be fulfilling can lead to suffering. Studies show that an "obsessive passion" for work leads to higher rates of burnout and work-related stress. Researchers have also found that lifestyles that revolve around work in countries like Japan are a key contributor to record-low fertility rates. And for young people in the United States, inflated expectations of professional success help explain record-high rates of depression and anxiety. Globally, more people die each year from symptoms related to overwork than from malaria.

Research aside, we know intuitively that sky-high expectations are a recipe for disappointment. When we expect work to help us self-actualize—to constantly motivate and fulfill us—settling for anything less can feel like a failure. A job, like a baby, is not always something that you can control. Tethering your sense of self-worth to your career is a perilous game.

And yet, the antidote is not as simple as to not care about your job. The average person will spend a third of their life—roughly eighty thousand hours—working. How we spend those hours matters. The question, then, is how to balance the pursuit of meaningful work with the risk of letting your job subsume who you are.

For that, we can turn again to the wisdom of Dr. Winnicott.

Compared to perfection, "good enough" is a more forgiving ideal. It doesn't romanticize what a job can offer, nor accept that work must be endless toil. *Good enough* is an invitation to choose what sufficiency means—to define your relationship to your work without letting it define you.

During my senior year of college, I had the opportunity to interview my favorite writer, a poet named Anis Mojgani. At the time, Mojgani was at the top of his game, having just won back-to-back titles at the National Poetry Slam. Mojgani was the first person I had ever met who was able to make a living from writing and performing. He traveled the world to speak at college campuses and open for musicians. He was my professional idol, a verifiable rockstar of rhymes. I was a twenty-two-year-old poetry student about to embark on a journey into an unknown future. I was convinced Mojgani would give me the "follow your passion" pep talk I thought I needed. He didn't.

When I asked Mojgani whether he believed in the whole "love what you do and never work a day in your life" mantra, he said something I'll never forget: "Work will always be work. Some people work doing what they love. Other people work so that they can do what they love when they're not working. Neither is more noble."

That last sentence shook me. Until that day, I'd believed figuring out what to do for work was life's ultimate mission. I had interpreted Annie Dillard's famous words—"How we spend our days is, of course, how we spend our lives"—to mean that my chosen work would define not just what I did, but who I was. But here was my professional crush, a professional poet no less, telling me that it's fine to have a day job.

I recently learned that Dillard's often-quoted line was never meant to become a mantra for hustle culture or a justification for the endless pursuit of one's dream job. In fact, if you read the rest of the passage from which the excerpt is taken, Dillard's point is to the contrary. "What we do with this hour, and that one, is what we are doing," she writes. "The life of the spirit requires less and less; time is ample and its passage sweet." Her words are a call for presence, not for promotions.

A life completely consumed by work crowds out other aspects of ourselves. In the words of psychotherapist Esther Perel, too many people bring the best of themselves to work, and bring the leftovers home. When we give all of our energy to our professional lives, we deprive the other identities that exist within each of us—spouse, parent, sibling, neighbor, friend, citizen, artist, traveler—of the nutrients to grow.

Much as an investor benefits from diversifying their investments, we, too, benefit from diversifying our sources of identity and meaning. Meaning is not something that is bestowed upon us. It's something we create. And as with any act of creation, it requires time and energy—the time to invest in nonwork pursuits and the energy to actually do so.

Here's how this book works. In each chapter you'll meet a worker from a different industry—a Michelin-star chef, a Wall Street banker, and a software engineer who lives in a van in the Google parking lot, to name a few. Through each of their stories, we'll examine a common myth that pervades modern work culture. From "this company is like a family" to "do what you love and never work a day in your life," many of the axioms of the working world become fuzzy and gray upon closer inspection.

What distinguishes this book from other career or business books you may have read is that the chapters primarily tell people's stories. You won't find any pages with three easy steps to separate your self-worth from your work, or ten quick tips to keep you from lying awake obsessing over your next performance review. My goal is that you'll treat this book less like a textbook and more like a mirror. That is to say, I hope this book prompts you, as writing it did for me, to examine your own relationship to your job. Each person's journey challenged my assumptions and helped me define the role I wanted work to play in my life. I hope the same will be true for you.

The stories that follow live in the tension between seeing

work as a means to an end and seeing work as the end itself—as historian Studs Terkel put it, the search "for daily meaning as well as daily bread." Defining our relationship to work is an on-going process—something we wrestle with every time we decide whether to spend an extra hour at the office or to check our email on a Sunday. This book is not a credo against seeking fulfillment from work, nor is it an argument for treating work as a necessary evil. It's a guide to developing a healthier relationship to work through the stories of people who have struggled to do so.

Developing a healthier relationship to work is not as simple as quitting your job or taking up knitting. Not everyone has the ability to dictate their hours or choose their profession. What we can control, however, are the expectations we place on our jobs. We can choose to subordinate work to life, rather than the other way around. It starts with a simple acknowledgment: you aren't what you do.

# The Good Enough Job

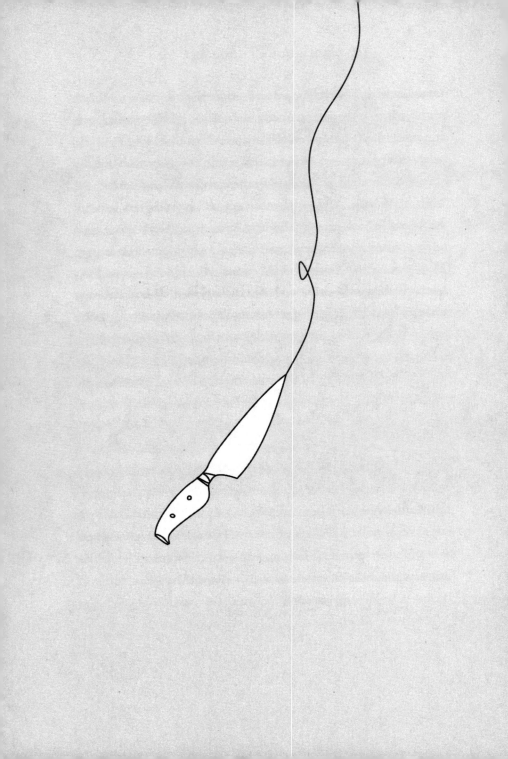

# 1

# For What It's Worth*

## On the myth that we are what we do

*Sufficiency isn't two steps up from poverty or one step short of abundance. It isn't a measure of barely enough or more than enough. Sufficiency isn't an amount at all. It is an experience, a context we generate, a declaration, a knowing that there is enough, and that we are enough.*

BRENÉ BROWN

Divya Singh was sitting in her college dorm room when her roommate's boyfriend said something that changed her life: "You couldn't get an internship at The Restaurant even if you tried." Divya was a nineteen-year-old Indian American culinary school student with sleek bangs and a single pronounced dimple

---

* Author's note: This chapter is based on true events. Names and identifying characteristics have been changed to protect the privacy of the individuals involved. Quotes from the arbitration proceeding are excerpted from the real transcript. Stephen Fischer's team declined to comment on the events in question.

under her left cheek. She was studying to become a nutritionist. Her dream was to design recipes for a glossy food magazine like *Bon Appétit* or *Saveur*, but that comment changed things. Cody, the boyfriend, was a tall, confident Midwesterner on the fine-dining track. Even as a student, he assumed the bravado common among male chefs. Little did he know, Divya was the wrong person to be told what she couldn't accomplish.

Every year, one student from the culinary school Divya and Cody attended was awarded an internship at The Restaurant, which was widely considered to be one of the best in America. It had just received three Michelin stars, another accolade for its famed chef, Stephen Fischer, whose home adjoined The Restaurant's kitchen.

The internship would be awarded by Randy Garcia, a faculty member at Divya's culinary school who used to work at The Restaurant. Garcia evaluated prospective students on their knife skills, solicited feedback from places where they had worked, and conducted interviews with each applicant. Divya had never worked in fine dining. But after she set her sights on The Restaurant, she spent the rest of her nights and weekends of the school year working in high-end kitchens.

At the end of the year, Divya and Cody both applied for The Restaurant's internship. Divya got it. Garcia told me she was the most prepared student he had ever recommended for the role. Even after securing the position, Divya continued to go to Garcia's classroom to practice chopping onions, carrots, and celery in anticipation of the summer ahead.

The Restaurant is a picture of culinary sophistication. The rustic stone building was a turn-of-the-century saloon before becoming a restaurant in the 1970s. When Fischer remodeled the kitchen, he told the architects that he wanted The Restaurant to resemble the Louvre—a mix of the historic and the contemporary. Every detail—from the cerulean front door to the "Sense of Urgency" sign that hangs below the kitchen's Vacheron Constantin clock—carries Fischer's fingerprint. The nine-course prix-fixe menu is $350 dollars a head.

Most fine-dining kitchens are organized by the so-called brigade system, made popular by a nineteenth-century French chef who based it on the hierarchy of European military kitchens. The head chef barks orders that the rest of the kitchen staff dutifully follow. Fischer, whose father was a Marine, implemented the brigade system at all his restaurants. As a commis, or junior chef, Divya was at the bottom of the pyramid. Everything in her first six months was "yes, Chef" or "no, Chef."

Divya's days passed in a blur of minced tarragon leaves and diced chanterelles. The chefs routinely examined the symmetry of the commis's cuts, and if they weren't up to their standards, the food would be thrown away. Working as a cook at The Restaurant was like working as an animator at Pixar or a cellist at the Vienna Philharmonic—being among the best of the best was intoxicating. But the work was grueling. "Your time there is the equivalent of dog years," a former general manager told me. "For every year you're there, it's seven years off your life."

At the end of the internship, Divya was invited to stay on, but she wasn't excited by the monotony of cooking on the line and wanted to graduate from school. So, she went back to finish her studies and devised a plan to return to The Restaurant on her own terms.

In the mid-aughts, molecular gastronomy was all the rage. Divya read about European restaurants with their own research and development kitchens, which used food science and chemistry to develop novel cooking techniques. Because The Restaurant changed its menu every day, the chefs often didn't have time to experiment with the most cutting-edge methods. So during her senior year of culinary school, Divya wrote her own job description and, at twenty-two, was hired as The Restaurant's first ever R&D chef. A few months after graduation, she was back at The Restaurant, experimenting with how to make seawater sorbet and turn béchamel sauce into foam.

One of Divya's responsibilities as the R&D chef was to create menu items for people with dietary restrictions. She spent months developing recipes for dairy-free alternatives to The Restaurant's signature tapioca pudding and leek soufflé. The R&D kitchen was housed in a separate building from the main dining room, but occasionally The Restaurant guests would ask to meet the wizard behind their dairy-free delights. One time, a woman who hadn't eaten dairy in seven years broke down crying in front of Divya while describing what it felt like to bite into her dairy-free brie. Divya knew she was onto something.

Divya saw a business opportunity to bring what she had learned in The Restaurant's R&D kitchen to home chefs. Most dairy-free alternatives require home chefs to substantially alter their favorite family recipes. Divya's idea was to create a line of dairy-free products that home chefs could substitute into almost any recipe. She decided to call it Prameer—a play on paneer, the Hindi word for cheese.

Since Divya was still on staff at The Restaurant, she didn't want her project to be seen as a conflict of interest. She set up a meeting with Chef Fischer to ask for his permission to start Prameer as an independent venture.

On the day of the meeting, Divya wore her starched white chef's coat, her hair pulled back in a tight ponytail. Divya and Fischer had never met one-on-one. Her heart was pounding as she sat on the picnic bench outside Fischer's office while she waited for him to emerge. A twenty-four-year-old recent culinary grad, Divya was about to meet with one of the top chefs in the world. *Who am I for Stephen Fischer to even care about?* she thought.

Just like she'd done for her internship, Divya overprepared. She brought research on trends in dairy-free baking and charts analyzing the competitive landscape. But when broad-shouldered Fischer stepped outside to meet her, he greeted her with the disarming charm of a college professor. "No need to be nervous," he said, flashing a smile. "It's just me."

After her pitch, Fischer didn't just give Divya the green light—he did one better. "What if I help you?" he asked. Divya was shocked. She had been grateful for just a half hour of his time, but now Stephen Fischer wanted to help *her*. "I don't need anything, but I'm just compelled to help you because you seem like a very driven, ambitious woman," he said. "Why don't we partner on this?" Divya came into the meeting with an idea and left with a business partner. They agreed to a fifty-fifty ownership split.

Over the next few years, Fischer took Divya under his wing. Despite being a notoriously busy man who ran several other restaurants with a constellation of Michelin stars, Fischer went out of his way to make himself available to Divya. They met regularly to talk about the future of the business. They appeared together in the glossy magazines where Divya had once dreamed of working. Divya ran the day-to-day operations of Prameer, but Fischer, who had no kids of his own, offered her advice and guidance. "This was the first time I ever had a mentor," Divya told me. "Like a father figure."

One day, Divya was feeling particularly anxious about the business, so she went to Fischer's office, which is a garden path away from The Restaurant's front door. After she talked through her worries, he said something that will forever remain etched in Divya's memory: "Hey, I just want you to know I'm really proud of you," he said. After the meeting, Divya went directly to her car in the parking lot. From the safety of the driver's seat, she started to cry. No one had ever told her that before.

As Prameer grew, Divya grew into her confidence as CEO. She'd developed the products, created the brand, and managed a team of a half dozen employees. The product hit the shelves with favorable reviews everywhere, from dairy-free food blogs to *The New York Times*.

The following year, *Forbes* included Divya, now twenty-six, on its annual 30 Under 30 list. The company was growing quickly. It launched in hundreds of stores across the country and expanded its product line to include dairy-free ice cream and yogurt.

But with the growth came strains on Divya's relationship with Fischer. After the business got off the ground, Fischer started to pull back, making Divya go through the restaurant group's chief financial officer to reach him. Divya wanted to raise funding from investors who had experience working with packaged goods brands, but Fischer didn't want to dilute ownership of the company. For every investor they brought in, Divya and Fischer would have to cede some power.

Instead, the company hired a new member for their leadership team, a middle-aged food executive who had experience working with large brands. Divya and the new hire did not get along. She felt that he patronized her and didn't trust her leadership as the company's CEO. But when Divya suggested they let him go, Fischer told her she was "being a brat."

Six years in, Prameer was doing better than ever, but Divya was not. The company was expanding into major retailers such as Whole Foods and Costco. But Divya felt distant from Fischer and exhausted from the time and effort she had poured into the business. She sought support from experienced food entrepreneurs, but every time she brought in a potential adviser, Fischer turned them away. Fischer didn't understand why Divya wanted to go outside of The Restaurant's inner circle for advice, and Divya didn't understand why he wasn't open to support that might help the company grow.

In another effort to expand Prameer's offerings, Divya and the team were developing an egg substitute product. The company signed contracts with retailers and began manufacturing, but less than two months before launch, Fischer started to get cold feet. He was unhappy with the design of the new product's packaging, which de-emphasized the company's connection to The Restaurant—a choice Divya had made to appeal to new customers.

Fischer decided to veto the egg alternative altogether. It was Divya's last straw. One by one, she called the vendors and distributors with whom she had spent months negotiating deals. As much as she wanted to believe that this was her company, it was never fully hers. Divya set up a meeting with Fischer to hand in her resignation.

In the meeting, Divya told Fischer she had lost the passion that inspired her to start Prameer, and although it was a difficult decision, she wanted to leave the company. Then Divya saw a side of Fischer she'd never seen before. He told her that she was being ungrateful, that she was squandering the opportunity he had given her. He raised his voice as his eyes narrowed. "I hope you know you would be nothing without me," he said. "You'd be nobody. You'd still be in that kitchen."

To a certain extent, Divya believed him. Even as her business partner and mentor berated her, she still felt beholden to his support. Divya agreed to keep working for the company for several months even after resigning. She still felt grateful to Fischer for his mentorship and kindness. "That was my frame of mind for years," she told me. "And I think in many ways that created a blind spot . . . I was blinded by feeling so indebted to this person."

After spending seven years nurturing Prameer from an idea into a successful business, Divya finally left the company. At first, the transition was rough. "I was left with this gaping hole in my identity," she told me. "I didn't know who I was without this job." She was so depleted that she felt physically incapable of doing anything else. But it was during this period of not working that Divya inadvertently started to build back her sense of self.

~ℓ~

Divya spent six weeks traveling alone in Thailand, a place where no one saw her as Stephen Fischer's right-hand woman. When she returned home, she began to explore some of the hobbies she had brushed aside during the seven years she built the business. She spent weekends camping in redwood forests and weekdays surfing on the coast. She taught herself how to skateboard and rediscovered the joy of cooking for pleasure.

"I was able to develop myself in different ways," she told me, "because I had the space to." She was no longer just a worker. She was a skateboarder and a sketcher, a community builder, and a thirty-year-old prankster. She loved to kidnap her friends and bring them to secret locations around town, go rock climbing in Halloween costumes, and show her housemates how to make samosas from scratch.

Psychological research shows that when we invest, as Divya did, in different sides of ourselves, we're better at dealing with setbacks. In contrast, the more we let one part of who we are define us, the less resilient we are to change. For example, in one study, Patricia Linville found that subjects with a more differentiated idea of themselves—what she calls having greater "self-complexity"—were less prone to depression and physical illnesses following a stressful event. When people who had less self-complexity experienced a stressful event, it was more likely for that stress to "spill over" to other parts of their lives.

This makes intuitive sense. If your identity is entirely tied to one aspect of who you are—whether it be your job, your net worth, or your "success" as a parent—one snag, even if it's out of your control, can shatter your self-esteem. But if you cultivate greater self-complexity and distinct sources of meaning, you'll be better equipped to weather the inevitable challenges of life.

Overidentifying with just one aspect of yourself can also be dangerous. Take Junior Seau, a linebacker who played twenty years in the National Football League. He led his team, the San Diego Chargers, to a Super Bowl championship and was voted to a record twelve-straight Pro Bowls. But less than three years after retiring, Seau tragically committed suicide.

"When you grow up an athlete and you live in a world that praises you all the time . . . the frequency of praise that comes your way increases," Miles McPherson, a teammate of Seau's, told ESPN after his passing. "All that one day stops. But your body, mind and heart are conditioned to such a high level of excitement, adrenaline rush, challenge, and then you're like taken off the drug, cold turkey."*

---

* After Seau's death, medical examiners also found that Seau suffered from chronic traumatic encephalopathy, or CTE, a degenerative brain disease linked to repeated hits to the head.

Unfortunately, Seau's story is not an isolated incident. From professional athletes to military veterans, CEOs to supermodels, losing your professional identity can be a shock to the system—especially if you haven't had the time or made the effort to invest in other sources of meaning in your life.

Stepping back from Prameer wasn't important for Divya just because it allowed her to rest and recover from the stress of running the business. It also allowed her to explore who she was outside the context of work. Slowly, she freed herself from constant thoughts of Prameer and the desire for Fischer's validation. But a sudden phone call from a colleague put her healing on pause.

After Prameer, Divya started working with a legal adviser with experience in the food and beverage industry. He was reviewing Divya's paperwork, including her K-1, an IRS form that reports the financial details of business partnerships, when he found something striking. "The form says you have zero percent ownership of Prameer," he told her on the phone. "It looks like Stephen zeroed you out."

Divya thought there had to have been a mistake. The previous week, Fischer had reached out to wish her a happy birthday. In the press, Fischer went out of his way to make it clear that he and Divya were partners. She had spent seven years of her life—almost her entire twenties—building the company from the ground up. She had owned 50 percent of it from the start.

Standing on a windy train platform, Divya called Fischer. "Could there have been a mistake on the K-1?" she asked him.

"No," he responded calmly. "You left, and we had to refinance things."

"How could you zero me out like this?" she asked. "How could you take away a company that I helped build, that I poured my blood, sweat, and tears into?"

"I'm sorry, Divya," he said. "It's just business."

But for Divya, their partnership had been about so much more than just business. Fischer had been her first mentor. Even when they disagreed, she always spoke to him respectfully, as a line cook might to their chef de cuisine. But those three words—"it's just business"—shattered her image of the man whom she'd spent her entire career idolizing, whose Michelin stars hung from the range hood of his kitchen. The man who she thought she could rely on unconditionally. It was like family, until it wasn't.

"Stephen, the one thing you should know about me is that I won't go down easy," Divya said, with the same determination she had felt in her dorm room with Cody a decade earlier.

"Is this a threat?" he asked.

"No, it's just something you should know about me."

That was their last conversation before they saw each other in arbitration.

A judge, a stenographer, two teams of lawyers, and the restaurant group's CFO sat with Divya around the long wooden table.

Divya was the only person in the arbitration room who wasn't middle-aged and white. Fischer arrived last. Dressed in a blue suit and scarf, he walked straight up to the judge, as if he were greeting a VIP dinner guest. Ever the host, Fischer shook everyone's hand before sitting down.

It had been over a year since the conversation on the train platform. Afterward, Divya contacted several lawyers in hopes of finding someone to represent her. Again and again, she got the same response: "Are you sure you want to do this? Litigation is hard and no one comes out a winner." But Divya was determined. Her mom used to tell people, "Divya has certain lines. After you cross them, good luck trying to sway her."

Divya finally found a lawyer who was willing to take her case on a contingency basis, meaning he would make money only if they won. Even so, Divya poured her savings into paying the legal expenses, hiring expert witnesses, and covering the various other costs of protecting herself against a celebrity chef. While she grew Prameer in the early years, she had paid herself a very modest salary—especially by CEO standards. Now, she funneled everything she had into the case.

The proceedings lasted five days. Each side brought their own financial experts, with Fischer's team valuing Divya's shares at a fraction of Divya's team's figure. The lawyers presented their arguments, painstakingly paging through printouts of five-year-old emails and company documents. Both Divya and Fischer were interviewed and cross-examined for many hours. When they weren't at the front of the room, Divya and Fischer sat directly across from each other at the end of the table, as though they were sharing a meal.

Divya's attorneys alleged that Fischer had no basis for diluting her ownership stake in the company, and that he'd done so only because he thought he could get away with it. They believed Divya should be paid out in cash for her economic interest in Prameer as well as for the damages Fischer's actions had caused her. Fischer's attorneys alleged that dilution was necessary in order to invest more capital in the business. They believed Divya's ownership stake was not worth nearly as much as her team claimed. But ultimately, it was a matter of Fischer's word versus Divya's. Outside of the room, the controversy over the impending Brett Kavanaugh hearings—another case of his word versus hers—dominated the news cycle. But for that week at the end of summer 2018, Divya's and Fischer's whole worlds were contained within the four walls of the arbitration room.

At one point during questioning, Fischer interrupted Divya's attorney. "You're making her out to be some naive little girl," Fischer said. "[If she] was brilliant enough to develop a product that never existed before, then she certainly has an analytical mind that should allow her to be able to decipher what she's doing on a legal document." It was the same Fischer who emerged the day he told her she'd still be in the kitchen if it wasn't for him. For a brief moment, the facade of his Michelin-star charisma cracked.

A week later, Divya received bittersweet news. She had won the case; but rather than a cash settlement, the judge decided to reinstate Divya's 50 percent ownership in the company, which tethered her back to Fischer. After a decade subsumed by Prameer, all Divya wanted was to wash her hands of this chapter once and for all. Eventually, Divya and Fischer agreed on a path for her to leave Prameer. Divya wouldn't get the time back, but at least she was finally free.

I recently visited Divya at her home, a fourteen-person co-op in Portland. The house is a converted Victorian mansion with a dozen bedrooms nestled on a tree-lined street two blocks from Mount Tabor Park. Divya's roommates represent a wide range of ages and backgrounds, including a forty-year-old climate activist, a twenty-nine-year-old filmmaker, and a two-year-old named Walden. The co-op shares groceries and holds biweekly "family dinners," which the roommates eat around a gnarled oak table in the dining room. It was Divya's night to cook. As she pulled crispy roasted cauliflower and broccoli from the oven in the communal kitchen, I asked what she hoped others took away from her story.

"I want to remind people that you have to create value outside of work to protect yourself," she said, placing the charred veggies on the countertop. Before she left Prameer, Divya thought her value as a human was tied to her value as a worker—that it was a result of her fame, her wealth, or her attachment to Fischer. "That's how abuse happens," she told me. "Boundaries are crossed time and time again because you don't know your own value."

As Divya shaved Parmesan over the veggies with the deftness of someone who had spent years in restaurant kitchens, I asked what she remembered most from the period between when she first joined The Restaurant to when she finally cut all financial ties with Fischer over a decade later. At first, her answer surprised me. It wasn't finding out that she had won the internship, learning Fischer wanted to partner on Prameer, appearing in *Forbes*'s 30 Under 30, or winning the arbitration case. What stood out most to Divya was the brief period after she left the company when she *didn't* work—when her identity wasn't tied to her career at all.

As Divya's story shows, a work-centric existence leaves room for little else. During the years Divya was building Prameer, her job didn't take up just her best hours, but her best energy, too. But none of us is just one thing. We are workers, but we are also siblings and citizens, hobbyists and neighbors. In this way, identities are like plants: they take time and attention to grow. Unless we make a conscious effort to water them, they can easily wither.

Diversifying our identity is about more than mitigating the

shock of losing our job. We shouldn't do it just to avoid the sting of negative feedback or the disorientation of retirement. We should diversify our identities because doing so allows us to be more well-rounded people. It allows us to contribute to the world in different ways and to develop a sense of self-worth beyond the economic value we produce. And ironically, research shows that people who have hobbies, interests, and passions outside of work tend to be more productive workers, too.

Sitting in the kitchen that evening, it was clear that Divya had cultivated an identity through communal living. She'd recently gone to a music festival with her housemates, and was organizing an arts-and-crafts night for the holidays. She'd converted a corner of her room into a tea lounge with an open-door policy for people to drop by. Her housemates valued her for much more than her job title, the success of her company, or her proximity to Stephen Fischer. They saw her as a talented home chef, a lover of the outdoors, a creative party planner, and a generous friend.

Today, Divya is working again. She cofounded another food company and recently raised $4 million in seed funding. When I asked her what's different about entrepreneurship this time around, Divya hardly took a beat to think.

"I know my price," she said. "Because I developed my identity outside of work, there's a cost that if work cuts into it—if it ever costs me a larger part of my identity and my life—I know it's not worth it."

# The Religion of Workism

## On the myth that your job can be your God

*There is no such thing as not worshipping. Everybody worships.*
*The only choice we get is what to worship.*

DAVID FOSTER WALLACE

The minute he saw the chart, Ryan Burge's hands started trembling. It was his tell. Anytime his hands began to shake, he knew he was onto something. It was March 19, 2019, the day the General Social Survey released its 2018 data. Since 1972, the GSS has gathered data on trends in American society—from political views to beliefs about the existence of God. With a half century of longitudinal data, it's a gold mine for social scientists like Ryan.

Ryan was particularly interested in what the new data would show about his area of expertise: trends in organized religion. Historically, the vast majority of Americans belonged to a religious group. In 1990, only about 7 percent of Americans identified as either atheist, agnostic, or believing in nothing in particular. But recently the tides had been changing. The country's most popular religions were all losing ground while the "nones"—the catch-all term for those who do not associate with an organized religion—were on the rise.

Ryan has a round face and buzzed light brown hair. But his boyish appearance belies the wisdom he's accumulated in his thirty-nine years on earth. He speaks like an audiobook at 2x speed, his mind often racing faster than he can get the words out. He gets as excited talking about research methods as others might talking about their children or their favorite sports team. The day that the GSS releases new data is Ryan's Super Bowl.

Ryan had spent all day eagerly anticipating what the data might show. As he drove the hundred miles from the university where he teaches to his home in Mount Vernon, Illinois, he planned the formulas he would use to crunch the numbers. When he arrived, he fed his two young boys peanut butter and jelly sandwiches and drew them a bubble bath with his wife, all the while counting the minutes until he could head downstairs to his home office.

He knew exactly what he was looking for: how people's engagement with the seven major religions in the United States had changed in the last two years. After he ran the numbers, he saw it immediately: for the first time, there were more people who claimed "no religion" than those who claimed "Evangelical" or "Catholic." This meant that the religiously unaffiliated was now the largest religious group in America, accounting for nearly one in every four people. That's when his hands began to shake.

Ryan dashed upstairs to dry off his boys from their baths and then returned to his office. *I've gotta get this out,* he thought. At 8:48 p.m., he tweeted a chart on the rise of the nones to his six hundred Twitter followers and then read his sons a bedtime story. By the time the boys were asleep, the chart had already gone viral.

Ryan's chart would go on to make the front page of Reddit, amassing more than two thousand comments. *The New York Times* and *The Washington Post* both picked up the story. The rise of religious nonaffiliation was national news, and Ryan Burge, a small-town academic from rural Illinois, was at the center of the story.

But for Ryan, studying trends in American religiosity was not strictly professional. That's because in addition to being a professor, he is also a pastor at a small church in Mount Vernon called First Baptist. When I asked him how he answers the question "What do you do?" he avoided answering. "That's been the story of my life," he said. "I've never really fit in anywhere. I'm always a little too much of this to be that."

Unlike many pastors, Ryan joined the clergy for the money. During the spring of his sophomore year of college, he didn't have a summer job lined up. So when he heard about an opportunity at a church twenty miles from his hometown, he signed up to become a youth pastor. After graduation, he worked as a bank teller but couldn't stand the monotony, so he decided to pursue a graduate degree in political science. While in grad school, he began working as a pastor at a small church of about thirty retirees before joining First Baptist at the tender age of twenty-three. Ryan has presided over the pulpit for the seventeen years since.

Mount Vernon is a town of fifteen thousand people in southern Illinois, closer to St. Louis than Chicago. The city's top employers are a tire manufacturer, a Walgreens distribution center, and a Catholic hospital named Good Samaritan. First Baptist sits on a large plot of manicured land on the outskirts of town. The main building is a pointed slate structure that houses a sanctuary with a wood ceiling reminiscent of a ship's hull.

The story of First Baptist reflects the story of thousands of mainline Protestant churches across the country—namely, a story of decline. When Ryan first became pastor in 2006, fifty regulars came to services on Sundays and every seat in the three-hundred-person sanctuary was filled on Christmas and Easter. Multiple days a week, the church hosted Bible study, charity events, and neighborhood get-togethers. It was a social and philanthropic pillar of town.

Today, First Baptist has about a dozen regular worshippers. The church stopped holding services in the main sanctuary, opting instead for a smaller, linoleum-floored community room. The congregants sit in a circle of black folding chairs.

The lack of people in the pews has, at times, angered Ryan. "I thought of myself as a failure," he writes in his book *The Nones: Where They Came From, Who They Are, and Where They Are Going*. "I felt like one of those factory workers who got laid off after twenty years of hard work and dedication, wondering why my efforts weren't being rewarded." But when Ryan dons his social science hat, it's easy for him to reframe the situation. He knows what's happening at First Baptist is not necessarily a reflection of his efforts, but a reflection of a decades-long trend.

The decline of organized religion does not have a simple explanation. One person might leave a religious tradition because of a passionate theological disagreement. Another might leave because the Sunday service moved a half hour earlier. But it's clear that institutions like religious groups that once provided the infrastructure for many Americans to find belonging, purpose, and identity are losing popularity. But when these institutions fade, the human needs for belonging, purpose, and identity remain. The result is that people look elsewhere. And what better place to look than where Americans spend the majority of their time: the office.

Until the sixteenth century, the idea that work ought to be anything other than toil was pretty much unheard of in the West. The ancient Greeks saw work as a curse that prevented people from engaging in the more sublime and worthwhile pursuits of the mind and spirit. The Latin word for business, *negotium*, literally translates to "not-enjoyable activity." It wasn't until the German theologian Martin Luther came along that our conception of work's role in life began to shift.

In sixteenth-century Europe, the Catholic Church was making a fortune selling little pieces of parchment called indulgences, pardons for sin to citizens looking to buy their way into heaven. Though Luther was ordained to the priesthood in 1507, he objected to the practice of selling indulgences. In his mind, fate was predestined and spots in heaven were not for sale. Each of us was called to a station—the cobbler to his shoes, the blacksmith to his metals—so that we could best serve the Lord. Labor, then, was a divine calling—our toil sacred, even.

Two years after Luther was ordained, John Calvin was born. Calvin took Luther's sanctification of work one step further. Instead of simply putting our heads down because we ought to, Calvin believed hard work was a key trait of those on the path to heaven, the Elect. The ability to work hard and receive outward signs of God's favor (read: wealth) was evidence of one's eternal salvation. Therefore, following Calvinist ideology, if you wanted to go to heaven, you could—and should—find a job in which you could work hard. That is to say: you should find your calling.

As the German sociologist Max Weber notes in his book *The Protestant Ethic and the Spirit of Capitalism*, there is a common spirit between capitalism, an economic system that values profit, and Protestantism, a religious system that values hard work as the path to heaven. Weber argues that Calvinism—specifically the idea that your ability to be productive is an indicator of whether you're going to heaven or hell—is the foundation for modern-day capitalism. Together, an economic system that relies on continual growth and a religious system that idolizes labor form the perfect conditions for a society that worships work.

If he were alive today, though, a sixteenth-century pastor like Calvin might not recognize today's "prosperity gospel" preachers like Joel Osteen, who have made millions selling books on how to make money. The prosperity gospel is a belief mostly among American evangelicals that financial success is the will of God.

Every Sunday, Osteen appears before tens of thousands of congregants in a converted NBA arena in Houston, Texas, and preaches that faith and hard work will increase one's material wealth. According to Osteen, "It honors God to get to work on time, it honors God to be productive each day."

In his bestselling book *Your Best Life Now: 7 Steps to Living at Your Full Potential*, Osteen writes, "What you will receive is directly connected to how you believe." It's hard to think of anything more American than the ideal that faith will get you rich.

But even as thousands of believers tune in to Osteen's sermons each week, many Americans are ditching the pews. Ryan has some theories for why.

**No religion from 1972 to 2021**

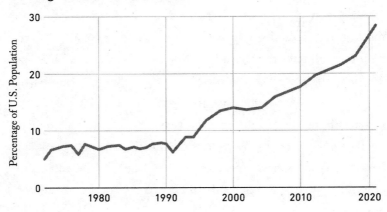

There are several prominent hypotheses about why people disaffiliate from religion, which together paint a picture of how the nones have more than tripled in the past thirty years. Ryan explained three of them to me. Looking at the chart above, it appears a seismic event occurred in 1991 that catalyzed the rise of the nones. Although there was no such event, the early 1990s saw the convergence of several social developments that had been bubbling for decades.

The first was the rise of the commercial internet. The internet made it easier for those who doubted their faith, like Sheila Connolly, to find each other. Sheila grew up in a Catholic home in Washington State in the 1990s. She was homeschooled as a child before attending Catholic boarding school as a teen and then a Catholic college. When she began to question some of the aspects of her religious upbringing, she felt alone.

If Sheila had been born a few decades prior, though, without access to the internet, she might have repressed her doubts and continued to partake in the traditions of her community. Social scientists have a term for this: the spiral of silence. When our views go against the social norms around us, it's easier to stay silent than speak out. Growing up, Sheila knew only one person who had left the church. But the internet opened up access to perspectives beyond Sheila's immediate Catholic bubble.

Online, Sheila found a community of others who shared her doubts, whose support eventually helped her build the confidence to leave the church altogether. "Churches can get books banned from libraries, but they can't make all the Google results fit their narrative," she told me. Sheila is far from the only one who has found a community of nonbelievers online. The Atheism subreddit has 2.7 million members. The Christianity subreddit, in contrast, has just 330,000.

Another common theory for the decline of religious participation is the politicization of religion, specifically the fusion of Christianity and political conservatism. Though the origin of the religious right is contested among scholars, the most commonly cited theory argues that, starting in the mid-1970s, a group of evangelical pastors who had gained notoriety as televangelists used their platform to lament the declining morality of American society. Using hot-button issues such as homosexuality, abortion, and pornography as key talking points, the coalition moved swiftly from the pulpit to the political stage. Scholars credit the Moral Majority, a political lobbying group founded by Baptist minister Jerry Falwell Sr., with securing two-thirds of the evangelical vote, a bloc that helped Reagan win the 1980 presidential election.

Concurrently, the fusion of religion with conservative political issues drove liberals away from the church. In 1972, 55 percent of white weekly churchgoing Christians identified as Democrats; 34 percent were Republicans. In 2021, 21 percent were Democrats; 62 percent were Republicans.

A third common theory about the rise of the nones has to do with increased social isolation. Americans simply participate in fewer social groups than they used to, religious groups being among them. In *Bowling Alone: The Collapse and Revival of American Community*, Harvard political scientist Robert Putnam studied social groups like bowling leagues and political membership organizations in order to chart the precipitous decline of Americans' collective social life. Putnam feared that the decline in social participation would fray the social fabric that binds us together, gives us a sense of purpose, and helps us feel like we belong to something larger than ourselves. He argued that faith communities were "arguably the single most important repository of social capital in America."

Ryan echoed Putnam's view. "Religion answers who we are in a social sense, not in a theological sense or in a psychological sense," he told me. "It's a Moose Club with a divine component." But with fewer Americans participating in community groups across the board, membership in both the clubs and the congregations is declining.

There is also a generational component to the rise of social isolation. According to a study by the London-based think tank Onward, by age twenty-five just 37 percent of millennials belonged to a community group like a church, book club, or sports team, which is down from 48 percent among Gen X at that age. As fewer members of younger generations participate in these types of groups, work has come to fill the void.

There are many possible explanations for why work, in particular, became a go-to replacement religion. Later on, we'll explore the rise of the "follow your passion" ethos, how the office became a hub for social life, and the deification of business executives. But the foundation of workism is the huge subjective value Americans assign to work. For many—especially college-educated professionals—work has become their primary source of meaning. But as Derek Thompson writes in his *Atlantic* article "Workism Is Making Americans Miserable," our desks were never meant to be our altars.

I learned the risk of worshipping work firsthand as a twenty-seven-year-old at a key juncture in my career, when I had to decide between two job offers. The first offer was for a staff writer position at a trendy online magazine. I had spent my twenties playing Goldilocks with careers—a few years in advertising, a few years in tech—all the while dreaming of writing full-time. I had done some freelance journalism on nights and weekends, but every time I said "I am a writer," it felt like a white lie. The staff writer position was the first job I'd ever been offered with the title to back it up.

The second offer was to be a designer at a prestigious design agency. I had wanted to work there ever since I heard the founder speak in grad school. "Work for this man!" I'd jotted in the notebook I kept tucked in my back pocket. A few years later, I had the opportunity to do so. It paid 50 percent more than the journalism job.

I waffled for weeks. I solicited the advice of everyone I loved. And my yoga teacher. And my Uber driver. I sought out a career coach. With the tacit endorsement of Michael Pollan, I even tried to see if psychedelics could help make up my mind. Zero progress.

Each time I made a pseudo-decision, I thought of all the reasons the other job was better. Maybe I should've gotten a job as a devil's advocate?

On one level, I knew how ridiculous my conundrum was: *Oh, the agony of deciding between two attractive job offers!* I judged myself for caring, for ascribing so much significance to the decision. But on another level, it really *did* matter. It wasn't just about my job; it was about my identity. It was about how I'd answer the question "What do you do?," which I took to mean "Who the hell are you?" It didn't feel like I was choosing between two jobs; it felt like I was choosing between two versions of me.

After weeks of deliberation, I took the job at the design firm. Actually, that's not the whole truth. First I turned down the job, and then, in a fit of panic, called the recruiter back the next day to say I'd had a change of heart. For the first few weeks in the new job, I was convinced I'd made the wrong choice. I took my morning coffee with a dollop of existential angst. I scoured LinkedIn, wondering if the journalism industry would ever take me back after my foray on the dark side.

I was insufferable. I was a crummy friend, unwilling to bother myself with the concerns of others. I was a crummy partner, incapable of talking about anything besides my own career questioning. And ultimately, I was a crummy worker, unable to think about anything other than my own personal fulfillment.

But, gradually, something began to change. I wish I could say that I had some grand epiphany, but what helped the most was simply time. I loosened my grip on work and started to get back into my weekly routines. I played pickup soccer and read for pleasure. I went to the park with friends and cooked dinner with my housemates. At work, I tried to focus my attention on the aspects of my job that I enjoyed rather than dwell on the myriad other things I could be doing. More than anything, I stopped obsessing so much about my choice. I saw my job as good enough.

At this point, the trap of workism was beginning to reveal itself for what it was. For one thing, as Divya learned, devoting yourself to work might mean a lack of devotion to other meaningful aspects of your life. Then there's the fact that a job might not always be there. If your job is your identity, and you lose your job, what's left? But there's a third risk that is perhaps more ubiquitous and pernicious than the others: expecting a job to deliver transcendence creates a massive opportunity for disappointment.

One benefit of putting your faith in religion as opposed to a more earthly pursuit like work is that supernatural forces are out of your control. "The compelling reason for maybe choosing some sort of god or spiritual-type thing to worship," David Foster Wallace says in his iconic speech "This Is Water," "is that pretty much anything else you worship will eat you alive." Worship beauty or money or power and you'll be left feeling as though you never have enough.

I worshipped work, and as a result, settling for anything less than a job that was absolutely perfect felt like a failure. It was only by removing work from its pedestal that I was able to see my work as part, but not all, of who I was.

It was Sunday morning, which meant Ryan was at the pulpit. Earlier in the week, he had seen a Jeep commercial for its new line of Grand Cherokee trucks, which he decided to use as the basis for that week's sermon. The ad's tagline read "The Things We Make, Make Us." From his place at the front of the community room, Ryan told his small congregation, "We should not identify with what we make, but by who we are and whose we are." But in the back of his mind, Ryan was conflicted. "I believe, by and large, we *are* made by what we do," he later told me.

Ryan genuinely loves what he does. He derives so much purpose from his work that even now, at just shy of forty, the thought of retirement terrifies him. "I want to get to the pearly gates someday, and God's going to say, 'What did you do for me and what did you use to build the kingdom?' And I want to say I gave all of it," he told me. "I left nothing in the tank."

Since the night his chart went viral, Ryan's popularity has ballooned. He now has more than eighteen thousand Twitter followers and is a regular commentator on religious trends for *The New York Times* and NPR. Editors from major publishers are eager to publish his next book, and large research universities are asking him to speak on their campuses. Seemingly overnight, a self-described "dude in a little town in rural Illinois" has become a public intellectual. As requests to write op-eds and give lectures flood in, Ryan faces one of the great ironies of the twenty-first century: the reward for professional success is often just more work.

But as the pressure to produce intensifies, Ryan's faith counterbalances the demands of the market. Though the prosperity gospel links faith with business, most religious traditions actively separate divinity from productivity—as either a separation of time, as in the Jewish tradition of Shabbat; a separation of space, as in a monastery isolated from the rest of society; or a separation of behavior, as in the Islamic call to prayer, which halts all other activities five times a day. As spirituality researcher Casper ter Kuile told me, the call to prayer literally "interrupts the bazaar." The point is not to compartmentalize faith away from the rest of life; it's to remind us to hold values higher than commerce, even as we go about our days in a commercial world.

For Ryan, work-life balance doesn't look like the best practices you might read in a self-help article. He checks his email on Sundays, often eats lunch at his desk, and plays *Fortnite* with his sons on his work computer. The line between his work and his life is less of a firm boundary than a porous sieve. But Ryan is balanced in other ways. He is not just an academic, similar to how he is not just a Protestant, a father, a pastor, or a dude from a small town in Illinois; he is all of those things.

For Ryan, striking a balance means turning down lucrative speaking opportunities that would keep him from delivering his Sunday sermons and cheering at his boys' soccer games. It means choosing to stay in Mount Vernon so he can continue to invest in his local community rather than pursuing a job at a large research institution elsewhere. "Finding meaning from multiple parts of my life means that when a setback comes in one aspect, it doesn't sting as much," Ryan told me. Work is not the only thing he worships.

Religious traditions help answer a fundamental question: What makes our lives valuable? They offer practices, teachings, and a community with whom to formulate answers. But in an increasingly secular world, we must find other ways to answer that question for ourselves. Work provides one potential avenue. Much like a church, the office itself functions as a container. It's a container for work tasks, an identity, and a value system, measured by productivity, efficiency, and dollars earned.

I don't think work is necessarily a bad place to look for a source of identity and meaning. I certainly identify as a writer and derive meaning from the work I produce. But it's important to remember that the workplace is just one container with one definition for what makes a valuable life. Assuming one value system as gospel is to balance on a narrow platform, vulnerable to a strong gust of wind.

One of the benefits of, say, joining a bowling league, learning to play the guitar, or hosting a weekly potluck for friends is that they each function as another container. At the bowling alley, no one cares about your job title. As you learn your first chords, you don't have to aspire to be a rock star. Your friends probably don't value you based on your economic output. (And if they do, you could probably use some new friends.)

Research shows that living a meaningful life is not necessarily the result of how much money you earn or what job title you hold. In fact, workers with the same job title at the same company describe the meaning they derive from their jobs in vastly different ways. One common trait that researchers *have* found that correlates with meaning is high levels of what they call "self-determination." In other words, people are more motivated and fulfilled when they determine what they value for themselves.

I can't tell you what to worship. But I do know that when you don't take an active role in determining what you value, you inherit the values of the systems around you. And when you invest in multiple sources of meaning—when you, like Ryan, hold multiple definitions of what makes life valuable—you invest in yourself in a way no company, boss, or market can control.

# 3

# The Love of Labor

## On the myth of dream jobs

*I have no dream job; I do not dream of labor.*

CASEY HAMILTON, VIA TIKTOK

Two years before Richard Bolles published the international bestseller *What Color Is Your Parachute?*, he, like many workers in the recession of the late 1960s, was laid off. After serving as an Episcopal minister for fifteen years, Bolles was let go due to a series of budget cuts. Rather than jump right back into the workforce, he applied for a grant to travel around the country and speak to people about their jobs.

Over the course of that year, Bolles heard from many unhappy workers who were considering "bailing out" on their careers. "I always thought of an airplane when I heard that phrase," Bolles told *The New York Times* in an interview before he passed away in 2017. "So I would respond, 'What color is your parachute?'"

The idea that personal satisfaction is central to professional success was still novel at that time. Work was largely thought of as a means to an end. People worked to provide for their families or to be productive members of society. Loving—or even liking—what you did was not a priority.

Bolles disagreed. *Parachute* argued that work allowed you to "exercise the talent that you particularly came to earth to use . . . in those places or settings that God has caused to appeal to you the most." In Bolles's framework, the first step of a job search should be to determine what lights you up. "He talked about mission in life with a capital *M* and vocation in life with a capital *V*," his son Gary told me.

Originally *What Color Is Your Parachute?* came in the form of a photocopied pamphlet that Bolles sold for $5 out of his Bay Area apartment. The initial print run was only one hundred copies. Since then, the book has sold over 10 million copies and been translated into over twenty languages. *What Color Is Your Parachute?* is one of the most popular business books of all time, and Bolles's message—that your work ought to satisfy you by reflecting your unique skills and desires—remains the prevailing wisdom to this day.

Using the language of personal satisfaction in relation to work sparked a revolution. Though Bolles didn't use the phrase "dream job" in the original publication of *Parachute*, his book helped convince workers around the world to follow their passions. Workers began to search for self-actualizing work—and industries quickly cropped up to help them find it. As a result, love and meaning began to supplant security and stability as our highest professional virtues. In the fifty years since *Parachute*'s publication, mentions of the phrase "dream job" in books have grown by over 10,000 percent.

If workism is the religion, dream jobs are the deities. But there's a dark side of expecting work to always be dreamy. "The problem with this gospel—your dream job is out there, so never stop hustling—is that it's a blueprint for spiritual and physical exhaustion," writes Derek Thompson. "It is a diabolical game that creates a prize so tantalizing yet rare that almost nobody wins, but everybody feels obligated to play forever."

Fobazi Ettarh decided on her dream job at fifteen years old. She was leafing through the stack of books waiting to be checked back in at her high school library in Fort Lee, New Jersey, when an anthology of short stories caught her eye. Though Fobazi was an avid reader, she rarely picked up anything that diverged from her standard helping of science fiction. But she had some time to kill, so she thumbed to a short story called "Am I Blue?" by Bruce Coville.

In the story, a sixteen-year-old named Vince is wrestling

with his sexuality when he meets a fairy godfather. With a tap of his wand on Vince's eyelids, the fairy godfather grants Vince the power to see every queer person as a different shade of blue. Vince opens his eyes to see blue cops and blue farmers, blue teachers and blue soldiers, blue parents and blue children. For the first time, Vince realizes that he isn't alone in his sexuality.

The story resonated deeply with Fobazi. "I really thought that I was the only one who was dealing with this," she told me. But the book helped her realize that being queer wasn't a "horrible taboo that would send me to hell . . . it was just another fact of life."

"Am I Blue?" opened Fobazi's eyes to the world of queer literature—and to the role the librarians at her school played in her awakening. Every week, she nervously walked up to the library counter to check out new books, like a teenager buying their first contraceptives. But the librarians never seemed to judge her. In fact, they went out of their way to recommend books with queer protagonists, like *Annie on My Mind* by Nancy Garden and *Keeping You a Secret* by Julie Anne Peters.

"If one adult had said anything disparaging at that time, I probably would have been in the closet for another ten years," Fobazi told me. She wanted to help others feel seen just as her school librarians had helped her. So, Fobazi set her sights on becoming a school librarian herself. She had found her dream job and would do whatever it took to get it.

~ℓ~

From the moment we ask children what they want to "be" when they grow up, we exalt the dream job as if it were life's ultimate objective. "You've got to find what you love," Steve Jobs told a stadium of Stanford graduates in his famous 2005 commencement address. "If you haven't found it yet, keep looking. Don't settle."

But the conventional wisdom of following your passion can be misguided, even damaging. For those who have found a job that they enjoy, expecting it to always be a dream is a recipe for disappointment. Artist Adam J. Kurtz neatly summed up this rationale in the piece *Work/Life Balance*, in which he scratched out the second half of the "Do what you love and you'll never work a day in your life" cliché in favor of a new phrase: "Do what you love and you'll work super fucking hard all the time with no separation or any boundaries and also take everything extremely personally."

Our society treats those who haven't found a calling—who don't love what they get paid to do—as if they've committed some kind of moral failure. "The only way to do great work is to love what you do," Jobs proselytized at Stanford. "Life is too short not to follow your passion," read proverbs on Instagram and LinkedIn. However, the notion that we should always love our job creates outsized expectations for what a job can deliver.

It ignores the tedium that exists in every line of work, blinds us to the flaws a dream job may have, and creates conditions in which workers are willing to accept less than they deserve.

Many full-time library positions require a master's degree in library and information science, which typically takes two years and tens of thousands of dollars to complete. Consequently, aspiring librarians, like Fobazi, often enter the industry in debt. Yet for many, the privilege of being surrounded by books every day is a worthy trade-off. As one librarian I interviewed told me, "Librarians aren't made, they're born."

After college at the University of Delaware, Fobazi went on to get her master's degree at Rutgers. In grad school, she first tasted what she called "the industry's Kool-Aid." She learned how libraries were built on the ideals of being available and open to all. Her professors called the library "the last truly democratic institution." But these aspirations didn't always bear out in Fobazi's research and lived experience.

In a field that prided itself on inclusivity, Fobazi saw a glaring lack of diversity. At Rutgers, one of the most ethnically diverse universities in the country, Fobazi, who is Black, was one of only two people of color in her forty-person cohort. Outside of class, she learned how during the civil rights movement, libraries in the South chose to shut down rather than integrate—events that were conveniently left out of her grad school curriculum. Also left out: libraries that used discriminatory ID rules to prevent certain citizens from entering. Libraries weren't always the democratic institutions they often claimed to be, and yet no one was talking about it.

"In every field, you see the difference between the ideals, what the narrative is, and the actual ugly truth propping up the ideals that has to be erased in order to keep that narrative going," Fobazi told me.

In Fobazi's first job out of grad school, evidence of her industry's imperfections continued to mount. Fobazi's supervisor told her, "No one becomes a librarian to make a living wage." Another referred to an Asian colleague, the only other woman of color on staff, as "the diversity hire." During a period of living at home after grad school, a local librarian refused to let Fobazi sign up for a library card because she didn't believe Fobazi lived in the neighborhood.

From the other side of the reference desk, Fobazi saw a workforce that was often overworked, underpaid, and overwhelmingly homogeneous. The median pay for a librarian with a master's degree is less than $30 an hour, according to the Bureau of Labor Statistics. Four out of every five librarians is white. Fobazi was forced to reckon with the discrepancy between her image of libraries and her experience working within them. How could working as a librarian feel so different from the paragon of inclusivity her graduate school professors described?

But whenever the pedestal of the profession exposed its cracks, Fobazi reminded herself how she'd felt checking out her first books as a terrified teen. Libraries had made her feel less alone, and she was committed to passing that feeling on to others. She loved what she did—at least that was what she kept telling herself. But over time, the hypocrisy of an institution that was supposedly "open to all" became increasingly hard for her to bear.

From today's vantage point, the idea that you should follow your passion is so common as to appear self-evident. But it wasn't always this way. It was only in the last fifty years—roughly the period since *What Color Is Your Parachute?* came out—that

### Frequency of phrase "meaningful work" in books

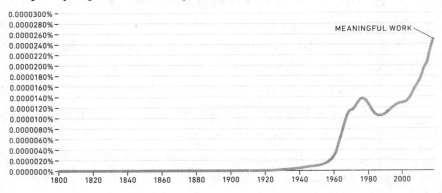

"meaningful work" even became part of mainstream vernacular. Before then, satisfaction was reserved for later—if not for the afterlife, at least for after workers left the office.

For the majority of the twentieth century the Fordist compromise—named, of course, after the policies at Ford Motor Company—defined the relationship between work and worker. In exchange for working eight hours a day, five days a week, Ford employees received decent pay, healthcare, some vacation, and a retirement plan.

These terms were further codified in 1941 when Ford signed its first collective bargaining agreement with the United Auto Workers union, which guaranteed workers standardized wages and greater job security. People accepted that work was an obligation, and enjoyment was sold separately. It was a premise that worked well—or at least well enough—when times were good. But as the buzz of the postwar economy faded, managers looked for ways to cut costs, and workers footed the bill.

As corporations shipped manufacturing jobs overseas and domestic wages stagnated, the job security and benefits of the Fordism era eroded. Since the 1970s, real wages—the value of dollars paid to workers after being adjusted for inflation—have barely budged.

"With dollar-compensation no longer the overwhelmingly most important factor in job motivation," William Batten, the chairman of the New York Stock Exchange, said in a 1979 lecture at the Wharton School, "management must develop a better understanding of the more elusive, less tangible factors that add up to job satisfaction." In other words, management needed new lures to keep employees happy. Management succeeded.

As we'll explore more later, companies like Kodak and IBM led the charge to brand the workplace as a hub for social activity and personal growth. In the second half of the twentieth century, flexibility, individualism, and meaning supplanted job security, workplace protections, and collective solidarity for many American workers.

But it wasn't just employers reshaping work's role. With the help of books like *What Color Is Your Parachute?* workers' tastes changed, too. A 1962 poll, for example, found that 6 percent of people thought meaningful work was important to success at the office. Twenty years later, the number was 49 percent. Today, nine out of ten people are willing to earn less money to do more meaningful work.

"It's become especially important that we believe that the work itself is something to love," labor journalist Sarah Jaffe writes in her book *Work Won't Love You Back.* "If we recalled why we work in the first place—to pay the bills—we might wonder why we're working so much for so little."

For librarians, the annual American Library Association conference is Mecca. Nearly twenty thousand librarians flock there each year. At the 2017 conference in Chicago, Fobazi was attending a panel discussion about libraries in schools when one of the panelists uttered a phrase that set off her alarm bells. The panelist told the audience that working as a librarian was a "sacred duty."

Fobazi knew about sacred duties. Her mother was a pastor in the Presbyterian Church. "The fact that we were using this word [sacred] to talk about our profession seemed so insane to me," she said. "I don't see how you can talk about how this work is holy, how this work is sacred, when there are all these problems that exist in the field."

Ignoring workplace malpractice is common in so-called labors of love. The idea that library science is a "sacred duty" is the same philosophy that encourages underslept healthcare workers to "put the patients first," underresourced teachers to "just make do with what you have," and unpaid college students to take an internship "for the experience."

Promoting the message that a profession is inherently righteous allows people in positions of power to characterize injustices as isolated incidents rather than systemic failures—if they're even discussed at all. Fobazi coined a term for this—vocational awe—and wrote an academic paper about its prevalence in librarians.

In the paper, she defines vocational awe as the belief that workplaces and institutions like libraries "are inherently good, sacred notions, and therefore beyond critique." In other words, the halo effect of the industry prevents people from seeing—or acting upon—problems that may exist within it. When workplace issues crop up, such as undercompensation, racism, or sexism, they are seen as isolated incidents rather than systemic flaws.

At the same time, job performance becomes dependent on how much meaning workers ascribe to what they do. "The problem with vocational awe is the efficacy of one's work is directly tied to their amount of passion (or lack thereof), rather than fulfillment of core job duties," Fobazi writes. "If the language around being a good librarian is directly tied to struggle, sacrifice, and obedience, then the more one struggles for their work, the 'holier' that work (and institution) becomes."

Fobazi published the paper in January 2018 in a small academic journal, but it quickly became clear that the phenomenon extended beyond her field. By the end of the year, Fobazi was being asked to speak at library science conferences and to guest-lecture at universities. From teachers to chefs, emergency room doctors to artists, hundreds of people reached out to Fobazi to share the flavor of vocational awe that existed in their line of work. In particular, responses flooded in from other do-gooder industries such as the nonprofit and public sectors, where the "privilege" to do the work is often seen as compensation in and of itself.

Perhaps no profession illustrates the vocational awe phenomenon better than zookeeping. Like working in a library, it's a job where the money is short and the hours are long. The majority of zookeepers have college degrees, but the average annual salary is less than $40,000 a year. The job is characterized by long hours, hard labor, and quite literally picking up shit. It's also a profession where the majority of workers have considered it a calling from a young age.

In a seminal study, organizational behavior researchers Jeffery A. Thompson and J. Stuart Bunderson interviewed hundreds of zookeepers about their relationship to their work. They found that the zookeepers' discovery of their calling came with a fair share of drawbacks. "A sense of calling complicates the relationship between zookeepers and their work, fostering a sense of occupational identification, transcendent meaning, and occupational importance, on the one hand, and unbending duty, personal sacrifice, and heightened vigilance, on the other," they wrote.

Many zookeepers framed their work as a duty, similar to the Calvinist conception of a divine calling from the previous chapter. As a result, choosing to work in another field would be more than an occupational choice; it would be "a negligent abandonment of those who have need of one's gifts, talents, and efforts," the researchers wrote. This exposed zookeepers to exploitation. Low pay, unfavorable benefits, and poor working conditions are often the sacrifices workers across industries must make for the privilege of following their passion.

"By cloaking the labor in the language of 'passion,'" writes journalist Anne Helen Petersen in her book *Can't Even: How Millennials Became the Burnout Generation*, "we're prevented from thinking of what we do as what it is: a job, not the entirety of our lives."

~ℓ~

A job will always first and foremost be an economic relationship. As Fobazi's paper pointed out, treating a job as something else—a passion, a sacred duty—diminishes workers' ability to call out and enact necessary changes. This has become particularly relevant in the past half century as workers have increasingly looked to work as an individual rather than a collective endeavor. But the shift from jobs as a source of stability to jobs as a source of fulfillment is also the result of broader labor market trends.

As GDP increased and wages stagnated in the last fifty years, for example, excess earnings have largely gone into the pockets of CEOs. In 1965, CEOs were paid twenty times more than their average employee. By 2015, CEOs were paid over two hundred times more than their average employee. "If you love what you do, it's not 'work,'" David M. Rubenstein, co-CEO of the Carlyle Group, one of the largest private equity companies in the world, told CNBC. It's no wonder the message from the top is that workers should work for more than money, when leaders keep the majority of the money for themselves.

Furthermore, jobs in historically unionized industries such as manufacturing have decreased while jobs in historically non-unionized industries like tech have increased. Employers adopt the language of personal fulfillment—"Change the world!"

"Do the best work of your life!"—to woo employees to these roles. But a thorny question remains: Is it really so bad to look to work for love?

Of course, many people love their jobs and still live happy, balanced, and stable lives. But when love and passion become stand-ins for fair pay, fair hours, and fair benefits, workers suffer. This tends to be particularly pronounced in industries with cultural cachet, like publishing and fashion, that often rely on the proverbial "line of people out the door that would happily take your job." From unpaid interns to adjunct professors who cling to the dream of tenure, those who follow their passion can end up in positions that amplify their vulnerability—especially for workers with less privilege.

"Not everybody has the same springboards and safety nets to parlay their passions into gainful employment," Erin Cech, a sociologist who researches fulfillment at work, told me. "If people are told to follow their passions, but we don't provide an equal playing field in which they can do that, then telling people to follow their passions helps reinforce inequality."

In passion professions such as teaching and nursing, where workers are expected to "not be in it for the money," gender- and race-based wage disparities are amplified. It's also worth noting that many of these passion jobs are also feminized and, by extension, devalued. Women made 83 cents for every dollar made by an equally qualified man in 2021. This gender pay gap widens for people of color. Black women are typically paid only 63 cents for every dollar paid to their white, non-Hispanic male counterparts, according to the National Women's Law Center.

The endless pursuit of dream jobs is at least partially to blame, according to Cech. If we believe that people make career decisions based on their passions, then it's easy to attribute wage disparities to individual choices rather than acknowledge the reality of structural injustice. This type of "choice washing" perpetuates the idea that income inequality can be overcome just by working hard rather than through systemic reform.

Furthermore, turning one's passion into a career is simply not attainable for most. In journalism, for example, most entry-level internships and fellowships do not pay a living wage. This creates a dynamic where entry-level positions go to young journalists who can afford to accept them, such as those with parents who subsidize their rent. Following your passion works best for folks with the privilege to manage the inherent risk of doing so. As Petersen argues in *Can't Even*, "Most of the time, all that passion will get you is permission to be paid very little."

It's not just workers looking for passion; employers are looking for passionate workers, too. From Starbucks to Goldman Sachs, Cech's research found that employers increasingly screen for passionate employees, even when passion isn't necessary to do a job well. "The job of a barista is making coffee all day long," Cech says. "So, the expectation that you perform passion when you're doing that job is additional labor beyond the immediate act of making the coffee."

Cech also cites an example in which employees at a local hotel chain were forced to fill in the blank "Hi, my name is [XYZ]. I'm passionate about _____" on their name tags. Performing passion this way is the spiritual equivalent of "service with a smile." Not only must workers be passionate about their jobs, but they're also asked to parade that passion around for the world to see.

During the COVID-19 pandemic, many workplaces pushed workers to their limits. Nurses were asked to take on additional shifts. Educators were asked to adapt to hybrid teaching. Restaurant workers were asked to put their health on the line. Workers were called "heroes" and "essential," but were rarely given additional protections or compensation. Vocational awe was on full display.

This was also true of librarians, many of whom were classified as essential despite their pleas to stay out of harm's way. Librarians across the country petitioned city officials to close the libraries and took to social media to air their grievances. "I assure you Chicago Public Library staff are bewildered, upset, blown away," tweeted Chicago librarian Amy Diegelman in response to the decision to keep the library open. "We are SCARED and ANGRY."

The library where Fobazi worked in New Jersey not only

decided to stay open but extended its hours until an executive order from the governor forced it to close. Before the governor's order, Fobazi, who is immunocompromised, was given permission to work from home, but she saw how other library workers and custodial staff were asked to keep going in.

In the name of public service, some of Fobazi's librarian colleagues were deployed to work at food banks and babysit for other essential workers. Thousands of librarians across the country were furloughed or laid off. At the same time, Fobazi's work critiquing the industry was in high demand. She was asked to speak about vocational awe at virtual conferences across the country.

Fobazi felt the cognitive dissonance of her career taking off while many of her colleagues were being let go. On one hand, the pandemic made plain the ways in which libraries and other institutions such as hospitals and schools relied on the perceived righteousness of their fields to justify their staffs' exploitation.

At the same time, hiring someone like Fobazi to speak at, say, the Association of College and Research Libraries (which she did) is the equivalent of an investment bank with a notorious culture of overwork hiring a work-life balance guru for a keynote presentation. Unless those in power back up rhetoric with policy changes, increasing awareness goes only so far.

Fobazi found herself at a familiar crossroads for activists: Would her time be better spent continuing to advocate for change from within, or should she take a step back to address vocational awe at a larger scale?

Initially, Fobazi felt grateful to still have a job as an academic librarian during a period of historic unemployment. Not only had she spent over a decade training for it, but it was also a tenure-track position, which afforded her a level of stability and security unavailable to the majority of her colleagues. And yet, Fobazi wanted to back up her beliefs with action. So, on December 31, 2020, she sent an email to her manager with her resignation. She decided to quit—not just her dream job, but also her career as a librarian.

"Part of the reason vocational awe is so dangerous is because it preys on the fact so many workers do feel a passion—if not a calling—for the work that they do," she told me. "Institutions rely on the fact that there will always be more passionate workers if the current workers leave."

Fobazi is now back in school, studying to become a professor of library and information science, where she hopes to push for library reform as an academic rather than as a practitioner. The fact that academia is another field where vocational awe is common is not lost on her. She knows the higher calling of "the pursuit of knowledge" and the promise of tenure can be used to justify unfair working conditions. At the time of this writing, graduate students across the country are striking for higher wages, expanded healthcare, and access to affordable housing. Fobazi has no delusions that this new career will be free of obstacles.

"I no longer have a dream job," she told me. "I'm going in with eyes wide open."

# Lose Yourself

## On the myth that your work is your worth

*If I could go back in time and give myself a message, it would be to reiterate that my value as an artist doesn't come from how much I create. I think that mind-set is yoked to capitalism. Being an artist is about how and why you touch people's lives, even if it's one person. Even if that's yourself, in the process of artmaking.*

AMANDA GORMAN

Every Monday afternoon, the staff of the *Jacket*, Berkeley High School's student newspaper, gathered in a large classroom for their weekly news meeting. It was the fall of 1999. JanSport backpacks. Skechers sneakers. Puka-shell necklaces. One such puka-shell wearer was Megan Greenwell, a sixteen-year-old sophomore who had recently joined the paper and was gearing up to write the second article of her life.

At these Monday meetings, student editors wrote story ideas

up on the chalkboard and assigned reporters to them. On one such Monday early in the school year, the staff of the *Jacket* discussed a piece of news from the weekend: the *San Francisco Chronicle* had reported that a seventeen-year-old girl, identified as Seetha Vemireddy, had died of carbon monoxide poisoning. "At the time, it didn't seem like it was a hot story," Rick Ayers, the paper's faculty adviser, told me. But since the victim was Berkeley High–aged and allegedly lived two blocks from the school, Megan volunteered to look into it.

Her first stop was the registrar's office. As the only public high school in town, most Berkeley teens—especially those who lived a few blocks from campus—attended Berkeley High. But when the registrar looked up Vemireddy's name, no enrollment records came up. Megan thought something fishy might be afoot.

Together with her news editor, seventeen-year-old Iliana Montauk, Megan began to investigate the story. They knew the victim was Indian, so the young reporters talked to South Asian students and faculty in search of a lead. No one seemed to know Vemireddy personally, but one teacher had an idea. The teacher suspected Vemireddy may have been forced to work as an indentured servant in exchange for passage into the U.S.—a known problem in South Asian immigrant communities in California at the time.

After two more weeks of shoe-leather reporting, consulting with media lawyers, and skipping class to follow the story, Megan uncovered something bigger than she could have ever imagined.

The victim was both a tenant and an employee of Lakireddy Bali Reddy, a sixty-two-year-old real estate mogul, who ran a modern-day slavery and sex trafficking operation. Reddy convinced young Indian women of the lowest social caste to come to the U.S. with the promise of improving their lives. Once the girls arrived, Reddy forced them to work for free under oppressive conditions.

On Friday, December 10, 1999, the *Jacket* ran Megan's story with the headline "Young Indian Immigrant Dies in Berkeley Apartment" and the subhead "South Asian Community Says 'Indentured Servitude' May Be to Blame." A month later, federal prosecutors charged Reddy and his son with trafficking and employing illegal immigrants and keeping the young girls as concubines. Reddy was sentenced to eight years in federal prison.

At sixteen, with the second article she'd ever written, Megan achieved the type of impact many journalists spend their whole careers chasing. *People* magazine called her "the high school Lois Lane" and *Good Morning America* invited her to appear on the show. The local chapter of the Society of Professional Journalists gave Megan the Journalist of the Year award.

Publishing that story didn't just give Megan praise and recognition, it gave her an identity: she was a journalist. "After that, it just sort of felt like, 'Well, I'm certainly not ever doing anything else other than this,'" Megan told me, "'and I have to be the absolute best at it.'"

To that end, Megan has, in many ways, succeeded. She was

the editor in chief of her college newspaper at Columbia University. Afterward, she got a job at *The Washington Post*, which sent her to Baghdad to cover the Iraq War as a twenty-three-year-old. She was also part of the *Post* team that won the 2008 Pulitzer Prize for its coverage of the Virginia Tech shootings. From the *Post*, Megan went on to write and edit award-winning features at *GOOD* magazine, *ESPN The Magazine*, and *New York* magazine, before becoming the first female editor in chief of the popular sports blog *Deadspin*. "It feels really scary and really stressful, and I also really like it," she told the *Longform* podcast a few months after accepting the *Deadspin* job. "Even the stress is energizing."

But the optimism didn't last long. Fourteen months after Megan accepted the editor-in-chief position, *Deadspin*'s parent company, G/O Media, was sold to a private equity firm called Great Hill Partners. Within two weeks of the acquisition, *Deadspin*'s new leadership fired twenty-five employees. Management attempted to institute a dress code and rules about the hours during which employees had to be at their desks. Megan and several other female leaders at the company were driven out and replaced by white men.

It was demoralizing for Megan to see the newsroom she was hired to lead gutted by new management. "The tragedy of digital media isn't that it's run by ruthless, profiteering guys in ill-fitting suits," she wrote in a scathing essay after she left the company. "It's that the people posing as the experts know less about how to make money than their employees, to whom they won't listen."

After *Deadspin*, in the summer of 2019 Megan was hired to be the top editor of *Wired* magazine's website, arguably the sixth dream job of her career. But it was from that perch at the top of the masthead that Megan noticed that something wasn't quite right. She didn't work particularly long hours—or at least not longer hours than she had worked in other jobs—but she came home feeling like "a broken shell of a person." It wasn't because she was working a lot. "It was that I wasn't capable of switching it off even when I wasn't working," Megan told me.

At the end of 2020, *Wired*'s editor in chief, Nicholas Thompson, left for *The Atlantic*. Megan stepped in as the interim editor in chief while the magazine searched for a replacement. While Megan was in the running for the full-time role, part of her was terrified that the company might actually offer it to her. She was burnt out. Editing stories, which Megan used to savor after long days of meetings, no longer excited her. She regularly had stress dreams about her job. Her husband—a doctor, public health researcher, and workist in his own right—was worried. On top of all this, her father had recently been diagnosed with kidney disease, and a pandemic was sweeping the globe. So in April 2021, less than a year after accepting the *Wired* job, she decided to take a break.

Megan wrote an email to her colleagues at *Wired* and bosses at Condé Nast. Anna Wintour, the esteemed chief content officer of Condé Nast, asked if there was anything she could do that might convince Megan to stay. Megan was flattered, but deep down she knew that no change in pay or role could erase her ennui. She respectfully declined Wintour's offer. At age thirty-seven, after working her way to the top of a competitive, male-dominated field, Megan dismounted the corporate ladder.

But for Megan, quitting was the easy part. The more difficult task was figuring out who she was when she wasn't working. For two decades, there had always been an article marinating in the back of her mind. Her life had run on journalism's clock; editors set her deadlines, and then, when she became one, Megan set deadlines for her staff. Most of her friends were journalists. When she wasn't at her day job, she volunteered as the director of the Princeton Summer Journalism Program, an intensive seminar for low-income high school students. Journalism wasn't just her livelihood; it was her life.

"I've always defined myself by my work, which means this transition has been far harder than I ever expected," Megan told me a few weeks after leaving *Wired*. "I'm flailing because I don't know who I am."

Psychologists use the term "enmeshment" to describe when someone's interpersonal boundaries become blurred. Enmeshment prevents a person from developing an independent self, as their personal boundaries are permeable and unclear. Imagine a kid whose self-worth is inextricably linked to his parents' validation, or a couple who are so codependent that neither person can make a decision without first consulting the other. Megan, like many ambitious professionals, had become enmeshed—not with another person, but with her career.

We are not born with a fixed identity; it's something we build over time. Much of our theory about crafting who we are comes from the German psychoanalyst Erik Erikson, perhaps the most eminent developmental psychologist of the twentieth century. Erikson believed people build their identities in stages through-out their lives, a key stage of which is adolescence. Our teenage years are ripe for instability. We grow physically, mature sexu-ally, and face important life and career choices. According to Erik-son, we solidify our identities at this critical stage in order to cope with all that's changing around us.

"This sense of identity provides the ability to experience one's self as something that has continuity and sameness, and to act accordingly," he writes in *Childhood and Society*, the book for which he is best known. Teenagers may overidentify with their favorite celebrity, or join cliques to gain a sense of identity by ex-cluding others. As we grow older, we continue to choose identi-ties as sources of stability. This was certainly the case for Megan.

As she was growing up, Megan's parents were both contractors—her dad in flooring and her mom in window cov-erings. Megan and her younger sister went to eight different schools between kindergarten and high school, as her parents moved the family up and down the West Coast in search of stable work. Megan says she had a bit of an obsessive personality, and she latched on to activities during different phases of her youth. In first and second grade, she entered national essay-writing contests. In middle school, she was an avid musical theater kid. In eighth grade, she became a competitive fencer. "I was super driven by external achievement and external recognition," she told me. Journalism, a career that provides a constant drip of urgency, competition, and recognition, was a natural fit.

In one of Erikson's most famous studies, he interviewed veterans returning from World War II. Like Megan after she left *Wired*, the soldiers were forced to reckon with their place in the world after they finished their jobs. For years, they had identified as soldiers. They knew the chain of command. Their roles and tasks were clear. Losing these things was tumultuous for them. Erikson coined the term "identity crisis" to describe the veterans' experience—a period of instability and insecurity that resulted from losing a critical part of who they were.

Identity crises were common among the ambitious professionals I interviewed for this book. Travis Cantrell, a former professional soccer player, felt as though he had to "turn off part of who he was" when he chose to retire from the game that he loved. Alice Walton, a startup employee who was laid off along with 50 percent of her coworkers at the start of the COVID-19 pandemic, told me, "It was really hard to not feel like I had failed at something," even though she knew that getting laid off was no fault of her own.

Ezra Fox, a video producer who was let go after seven years during a company reorganization, told me, "It's hard when you get information from the world that goes against one of the central narratives of your life." Ezra had conceived of himself as someone who was successful, a narrative that was reinforced by years of good grades and promotions. But being laid off spurred an internal reckoning for him. He couldn't reconcile the story that he was "successful" with someone who had just lost his job.

Social scientist Arthur Brooks argues that we're good at ascribing meaning to the narrative arc of our lives, but are often ill-equipped to react if the script changes. Breaks in the script—such as retirement, a sabbatical, or a round of mass layoffs—test our resilience. They require us to edit or, in some cases, throw out the old script altogether. But these breaks also provide us with an opportunity to start a new one from scratch.

Perhaps no group exemplifies the potential to rewrite the script more than people who are chronically ill. Often chronic illness cannot be anticipated or controlled. Some days you may wake up full of energy. Other days, you might not have enough energy to get out of bed. People like Megan, who tend to measure their self-worth based on their productivity, can learn a lot from those whose ability to be productive is often out of their control.

Take Liz Allen. Liz grew up as a competitive swimmer. In

college she competed as a Division I athlete in both swimming and water polo. But during the summer after her freshman year, she contracted Lyme disease. Within months, Liz went from swimming four hours a day to being bedbound in her childhood home, her mother spoon-feeding her chicken soup.

Lyme disease led to other health complications for Liz, including chronic fatigue and migraines. But over time, her health slowly improved. After college she got a job teaching sixth-grade science at a Colorado middle school. She loved the work. She was happy to get in early and stay late.

But during her third year as a teacher, the long hours and stress of teaching inflamed her already-sensitive immune system. She was forced to quit her teaching job—a job that had felt like a calling—because she was no longer able to spend a whole day in the classroom. Unlike Megan, who left work on her own terms, Liz's decision to stop working was not her choice.

"When you start losing 'I am' statements at the rate that I've lost 'I am' statements, it gets scarier to keep going," Liz told me. But she persisted. Liz found a community of people online who refused to let their chronic illnesses define them. She learned how to create new "I am" statements that weren't based on her output. "I am generous with my time, I am full of love, I am a good listener," she told herself. She started to define herself by her evergreen characteristics rather than by what she was able to produce.

"When you hit the bottom and you aren't producing or contributing in any of the ways society expects and capitalism demands, you look around and ask: Do I have value?" she told me. But with the help of the disability community, Liz was able to build other pillars of value beyond her output. So even if one pillar were to crumble, her foundation would remain.

Perhaps the most American "I am" label is "a producer." Workers are measured by their productivity, companies are measured by their growth, and the country's health is measured by its GDP. We celebrate those deemed to be "productive members of society" and call those who rely on social services "welfare queens" and "freeloaders." But it isn't just our country or employer that imposes this value system on us. Using productivity to measure worth is a standard we also impose on ourselves. And in the process, many Americans have internalized the values of our dominant economic system: capitalism.

From the twelfth to fifteenth centuries, Europe operated in a feudal economy. In the countryside, lords rented their land to peasants who, in exchange, worked and lived upon it. After paying rent, peasants sold what was left over from their harvest. In town, industries were organized into guilds with rigid hierarchical structures. Only men could enter the guilds, and only master craftsmen, such as blacksmiths or bakers, could produce within them.

One purpose of the guilds was to minimize competition. By limiting the number of bakers in town, for instance, the bakers' guild ensured the supply of bread didn't outstrip demand and cause the price to fall. For centuries, economies remained local, and foreign trade was rare. But that all changed at the start of the sixteenth century.

At the beginning of the 1500s, the new profession of the merchant capitalist emerged. Merchants purchased foreign goods cheaply and sold them to the European aristocracy for large profits. They persuaded craftsmen to sell them their goods and then traveled from town to town in search of the best price. This meant that craftsmen now competed with other craftsmen outside of their region. The market, rather than the guilds, increasingly dictated prices, and the guilds broke down.

Initially, merchants simply connected producers and consumers, but as their power grew they began to have a say in how goods were produced, too. Merchants commissioned orders from craftsmen in advance, provided them with raw materials, and paid them a wage for their labor. Rather than make money solely from trade as merchants, they now acquired wealth by controlling the means of production—as capitalists. This meant a major loss of autonomy for workers, as anyone who has ever been an employee knows.

When prices were fixed and customers were local, workers produced and sold only what they needed. As most work took place outdoors, the sun regulated working hours and the intensity of work varied with the season. In a capitalist world, however, those with capital regulated work. The more the ownership class drove down the cost of production, the more profit they would later reap. Owners were incentivized to pressure workers to work more for less. Workers, who often did not have the wealth to invest in the facilities upon which their work depended, succumbed to those who paid their wages. They were only as valuable as what they were able to produce.

In the eighteenth and nineteenth centuries, technological advances catapulted the world from economies based on handcrafts and farms to those based on manufacturing and factories. Rather than work in markets and fields, workers flocked to production lines that split jobs into repetitive tasks. As Karl Marx theorized, labor under industrialized capitalism alienated workers from the products of their work. Rather than make goods for their local communities, workers made goods that were shipped to places they couldn't see. This type of industrialized labor, according to Marx, estranged workers not only from what they produced but also from their humanity—from the communities and identities that made them who they were.

In today's economy, alienation assumes different forms. In 2017, U.S. surgeon general Vivek Murthy deemed loneliness a public health crisis. "We live in the most technologically connected age in the history of civilization, yet rates of loneliness have doubled since the 1980s," Murthy wrote in the *Harvard Business Review*. The reasons Americans are so lonely are manifold.

For one, many workers, like Megan's parents, have moved away from their hometowns and communities in search of better job opportunities. Add on the decline in social and religious groups, and you get a situation where, as Murthy goes on to explain, work has become many Americans' primary social circle.

Clearly there's a risk in relying on a single institution to fulfill so many roles in our lives. "With my work, I was really putting a lot of my eggs in this one basket," Ezra, the video producer, told me. "You're basically saying, this is my social life, my sense of purpose, this is also how I feed myself and my family, and, at any point, someone else can take that away from me."

I can relate to this. None of the fields in which I've worked— advertising, tech, journalism, and design—felt like clock-in, clock-out industries. There was always a happy hour to attend or a work-related text to answer after working hours. This wasn't always a bad thing. I genuinely enjoyed the company of the people I worked with. I made real friends.

But I also saw the risks of a work-centered existence. After days of interacting with few people other than my coworkers, receiving one piece of critical feedback made me feel like a failure. I saw my colleagues orient their entire lives around their jobs, only to be let go when the company faltered. I saw the risk of surrendering my fate to an institution with profit incentives.

Of course, when employees identify with work, it's good for employers. Countless studies have proven that higher levels of "occupational identity" among workers lead to increased retention, increased productivity, and more hours worked. "It's that community—being surrounded by a group of like-minded individuals, being part of something bigger than yourself—that inspires people to work harder, spend more time at work, and just have fun," WeWork cofounder Adam Neumann told the audience at TechCrunch Disrupt in 2017. But, as spirituality researcher Casper ter Kuile told me, "I don't think you can be in full community with someone who has the ability to fire you." Putting all of the eggs of our identity in the professional basket, as Ezra put it, is dangerous—especially when the basket reveals its holes.

Psychologist Janna Koretz, whose practice specializes in helping people with high-pressure careers, has found that increasingly more of her clients "delude themselves" into thinking they are only as valuable as their output. Koretz's clients are often people who, like Megan, have checked all the boxes. They've excelled in school and worked hard to advance in their career, but are left asking, "Is this it?" Koretz believes the reason so many of her clients feel this ambiguous sense of disappointment is because they've spent their adulthood so focused on climbing ladders that they feel lost when there aren't more rungs to grab.

In this way, American work culture often perpetuates a chicken-and-egg problem. People work all the time, so they don't know what to do when they aren't working. And people don't know what to do when they aren't working, so they work all the time. We treat weekends as if they were apart *from* our lives rather than a part *of* our lives. Even the language we commonly use for rest—unplug, recharge—presumes rest is simply a prerequisite for getting back to work.

To escape this loop, Koretz recommends two practices. The first is to intentionally carve out space for nonwork time. Rabbi Abraham Joshua Heschel described Shabbat, the weekly practice of Jews abstaining from work, as "a cathedral in time." Similarly, Koretz recommends building infrastructure around sacred time as one might build infrastructure around sacred space like a temple, mosque, or church.

A time sanctuary can take many forms—an hour a day with your phone in airplane mode, a weekly hobby date with a friend—but regardless of what it looks like or when it is, Koretz believes it's important to designate time when work is not an option. One of the benefits of, say, going to church or a yoga class is that it's impossible to work while you're there. Although many of us intend to work less, work seeps back in unless we actively protect time away from it.

Koretz also recommends trying on different identities for size. In order to build a more resilient sense of self, she advocates for actively investing in our nonwork identities. Put simply, if we want to understand who we are when we're not working, we must *do* things other than work. According to Koretz, developing a sense of self outside of work starts by giving yourself permission to try something new and not be "good." "I see all of these ambitious people, so when they think about investing in something outside of work, they want to sign up for a marathon," she told me. "But that's just another recipe for burnout. I tell people to start small: How about a run?"

Goal-oriented hobbies like signing up for a marathon or reading a certain number of books in a year can provide accountability to do things outside of work. But striving for a goal still imposes a frame of improvement, which implies work in a fundamental sense. This isn't to say these types of hobbies are bad. But I can't help thinking that, through all of our quantified ambition, we lose sight of the wisdom we all knew as children: the joy of play.

Play is a natural antidote to workism. It indexes not on utility, but on curiosity and wonder. It cares not about "better," but only about our present experience. Like rest, play can be a source of rejuvenation. And there are opportunities to play all around us. In art, there's crafting. In music, there's jamming. My personal favorite is dancing. The closest I get to the enthusiasm of a child on a playground is on the dance floor at a wedding. Play helps us remember that we exist to do more than just produce.

A few years back, Megan was slightly stoned, sitting on a beach with her younger sister on the Oregon coast, when her sister asked her a question: "How does it feel to be professionally accomplished?" The question caught Megan off guard. She had never really considered herself professionally accomplished. She told me that it wasn't until 2017—almost two decades after she won her first journalism award—that she first felt that if she lost her job she'd be able to get another one. Sure, she knew she had accomplished some things, but she didn't *feel* accomplished. In true journalistic form, Megan answered her sister's question with one of her own. "How does it feel to have an identity outside of what you do for a living?"

Megan admits she envies her sister, who makes good money working in marketing for a credit rating agency, stops work at five p.m., and has hobbies and friends who aren't her colleagues. "Her work always seems incredibly enviable to me, like being an NBA player feels enviable to me—it's just not a life I'm ever going to live," Megan told me. But it's not her sister's job that Megan desires—it's her sister's *relationship* to her work that appeals to her. Even after Megan began a self-imposed sabbatical after *Wired*, she found it difficult to detach from her professional identity.

Within a month into her sabbatical, Megan realized that her problem went deeper than her job description. "What the last month has shown me really clearly is that there's actually something much more fundamental about my relationship with work that is unhealthy," Megan told me. Like Liz, she had to teach herself how to not conflate what she produced with who she was. "It's hard and valuable in equal measure."

There's a saying in the Alcoholics Anonymous literature that you can't think yourself to better action, you've got to act yourself to better thinking. Figuring out who you are when you're not working is a practice. It requires letting go of the control, validation, and comfort of a work-centric existence in order to ask a hard question: Who are you when you're not producing?

It's still not an easy question for Megan to answer. When she decided to take a sabbatical, Megan had money saved. Her partner was still working full-time. She had plenty of runway before she needed to go back to work. But in the first few months, every time she started to relax, she felt the urge to be productive— to either figure out her next step or write a book proposal. But then every time she followed her urge to work, she felt guilty for not relaxing.

She took walks in the Catskills to clear her mind and inevitably found herself ruminating on a feature story she wanted to pitch or mulling over an idea for a new media business model. She was still caught in the vicious cycle that's all too common among workers today. In a culture that valorizes side hustles and career advancement, the message is that if you aren't getting ahead, you're falling behind.

On a blustery February morning, I traveled to Brooklyn to meet Megan at a café near her Williamsburg home. It had been nine months since Megan stepped away from full-time employment— one of the perks of her now flexible schedule being the ability to grab a coffee at eleven a.m. on a Monday. It was one of those sideways-rain, snow-turning-to-mush Northeast days, so we shuffled with our warm drinks to a transparent enclosure reminiscent of an oversized plastic umbrella. Through chattering teeth and visible breath, I asked Megan if the sabbatical had changed her in any significant way.

"What it hasn't done is force me to develop a new identity outside of work," she said. "It hasn't necessarily forced me to develop a new hobby or discover a new part of myself." This surprised me. The headline of Megan's past year might have been "High-powered media executive *Eat Pray Love*s herself back from burnout; memoir forthcoming." But instead, from an enclosed parklet in Brooklyn, Megan shared no stories about spontaneous trips to Bali or solo visits to the Met on a weekday. Instead, I heard the voice of a goal-oriented professional still wrestling with the role she wanted work to play in her life.

"I do like work. I like what I do," she said as she looked out to the street, cheeks flushed from the winter cold. "But I do wonder what percentage of my drive to work all the time is that

I truly love it, and how much is that I don't know what else to do with myself."

Part of Megan's drive to work so much is fueled by money, though Megan characterizes this relationship as "irrational." She has an impressive résumé, an extensive network, and a supportive partner through whom she gets health insurance. But like many older millennials, she has had a front-row seat to the precarity of both her industry and the American economy during her two-decade career. She saw how, for her parents, the availability of work dictated where Megan and her sister lived and the number of Christmas presents that appeared under the tree. Her work ethic is at least in part driven by the uncertainty of her own employability, irrational as it may be. Even during a self-imposed sabbatical, work is still the primary lens through which she sees the world.

I asked whether Megan wanted another job right now. "I don't," she said almost reflexively. "Well, I don't, but there's one specific job that I think would be interesting," she added with a smile. In the wink of her voice, I could hear a tension that I've struggled with myself: the understanding that we *are* more than what we do and yet the desire to find a job that helps us self-actualize all the same.

Nine months after she left *Wired*, Megan still sleeps, eats, and breathes journalism. She still aspires to run another newsroom someday. She still nerds out about long reads and business models and tactics to bring more women into editorial leadership.

But, perhaps for the first time since she was a sophomore writing for her high school newspaper, she's taken her foot off the gas for long enough to find worth in other ways, too.

As we sat in the parklet, fingers searching for warmth in the bottom of our pockets, Megan told me about how taking time away from work allowed her to spend time with her dad while he was in hospice last fall. She told me about the Thanksgiving dinner she single-handedly prepared for a dozen family members after his passing. She told me that in the previous nine months she had been a better friend than in any other period of her adult life because "life didn't feel subservient to work."

"I've done a better job of bringing things into balance," she said with pride in her voice. "I learned how to turn my work brain off."

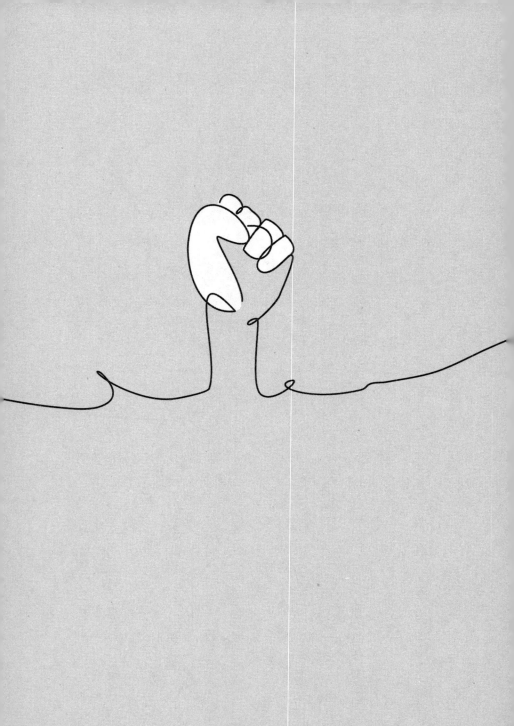

5

# Working Relationships

## On the myth that a workplace can be family

*The only effective answer to organized greed is organized labor.*

THOMAS DONAHUE

Taylor Moore looks like a young Santa. Scruffy beard, boxy build, the kind of guy who needs little prompting to tell a story around a campfire. "I'm a blowhard," he told me on Sunday afternoon mid-pandemic. "I don't really believe in astrology, but if we're talking about personality, I'm definitely a fire sign."

Taylor has the determination of a bulldog, which has served him well during the drunkard's walk of his career. Originally from Fayette, a small town in western Alabama, he spent his youth bouncing around the South. He tended bar, worked as an elementary school guidance counselor, and played banjo and guitar in a few Birmingham bands. By his midtwenties, he thought that if he didn't take "a big swing," he would die in

Birmingham—comfortably, but not really having *done* anything. So in 2006, he sold his car and bought a one-way ticket to New York City.

For his first few years in New York, Taylor took any job he could get. He was a dog walker, a bartender, a temp, a production assistant on indie-film shoots, and a nanny for a family on the Upper East Side. But the jobs were always a means of supporting Taylor's side projects. He spent his nights and weekends doing improv at the Upright Citizens Brigade and podcasting from the makeshift studio he set up in the closet of his Bedford-Stuyvesant apartment.

When the family Taylor worked for no longer needed childcare, a friend connected him to Kickstarter, a three-year-old Manhattan-based startup that helped artists raise funding for their creative projects. The company's mission resonated with Taylor, an indie creator himself. Through crowdfunding, Kickstarter enabled artists to circumvent traditional gatekeepers and tastemakers. Also, Kickstarter's founders seemed more interested in building a cultural movement than a traditional tech company. "Fuck the monoculture" became the startup's rallying cry. Taylor was hooked.

Like many young entrepreneurs in the early 2000s, Kickstarter's founders shared grandiose dreams of changing the world. They made it clear from the start that they didn't want Kickstarter to be like any other company. The founders vowed never to sell the company, and to measure success by the number of creative projects they helped bring to life, not the size of their profits. They asked employees to buy into this mission, which meant accepting less-than-market-rate salaries and forgoing the stock options that often convince people to assume the risk of joining a startup in its early days. In exchange, employees got to work for a company with a social mission, alongside coworkers with similar values.

The founders further enshrined their unconventional approach in 2015 when the company reincorporated as a "public benefit corporation"—also known as a B Corp—a legal designation that obliged the company leadership to consider the impact of their decisions on society, not just shareholders. Kickstarter pledged 5 percent of its profits to arts education and organizations fighting systemic inequality while remaining a for-profit company. Executives told employees and the press that they wanted to act more like a person with a conscience than a corporation that cares only about making money. Unsurprisingly, the company's creative, values-driven culture attracted an influx of creative, values-driven employees. They often hired people like Taylor who pursued artistic projects on the side.

In 2012, Taylor joined Kickstarter as a receptionist. He was, in more ways than one, the face of the company. He opened the door for visitors and welcomed them into the company's open-plan office on the top floor of a refurbished tenement building. Once a week, Taylor started a happy hour tab with the company credit card at a local bar. He hosted a midnight movie club at the office, where employees sipped negronis and watched cult classics. He played in a weekly Kickstarter Dungeons and Dragons game, which Perry Chen and Yancey Strickler, two of the company's founders, regularly attended. Kickstarter became the center of Taylor's social scene. Coworkers weren't just colleagues; they were friends and bandmates, romantic partners, and political comrades. According to a half dozen other early employees with whom I spoke, in its early days Kickstarter felt less like a company and more like a family—an ethos common within close-knit startups.

Some companies, like the British product development agency ustwo, make their desire to foster a family-like culture explicit. "Our focus has always been on building what we refer to as a 'fampany'—a company that feels like a family," reads the company's "cultural manifesto." Airbnb employees refer to each other as "Airfam." Salesforce defines its corporate culture using the Hawaiian word "ohana," which means "chosen family." At Kickstarter, building a family-like culture was never one of the founders' explicit goals. Employees hung out because they enjoyed each other's company, not because they had to.

But a family-like culture emerged nonetheless, which, according to Alison Green, the founder of the popular career advice blog *Ask a Manager*, can be a double-edged sword for employees. "Cultures that say their workplace is like a family are almost never to employees' advantage," Green told me. "It often means that you'll be expected to work for unreasonably long hours with an unreasonably high workload for unreasonably low pay, and that if you push back on any of those things, you'll be told either explicitly or implicitly that you're not being part of the family."

Regardless of whether a company's employees or executives say they're like a family, the sentiment can never be genuine. Families and businesses have fundamentally different goals. What companies generally mean when they say they're like a family is that they look out for their employees. Familial relationships, however, are unconditional. At-will employment, by definition, is not. Loyalty to the business will always supersede loyalty to employees. What companies and families do share is a tricky power dynamic—a lesson Taylor eventually found out the hard way.

On the surface, a close-knit office culture seems like a good thing. Research shows that people with friends at work are happier and healthier. One study from Gallup found that people who had a best friend at work were seven times as likely to be engaged in their jobs as people who did not. Employees with friends at work report higher levels of productivity, retention, and job satisfaction.

Employers have certainly taken notice. Many companies actively cultivate a sense of friendship and camaraderie through team-building exercises, free meals, and happy hours. Social and extracurricular events may help employees develop a sense of belonging, which has been proven to positively affect a company's bottom line. A study from the workplace coaching startup BetterUp found that a sense of workplace belonging leads to a 56 percent improvement in job performance, a 50 percent reduction in turnover risk, and a 75 percent decrease in employee sick days.

But for workers, relying on work as their primary social community is often fraught. Although employees with friends at the office tend to perform better, they also report being more emotionally exhausted and conflict-avoidant. In the paper "Friends without Benefits: Understanding the Dark Sides of Workplace Friendship," Wharton researchers Nancy Rothbard and Julianna Pillemer explain how some of the defining features of a friendship are in tension with the defining features of an organization.

In a friendship, roles are informal. Relationships are social and emotional in nature. In a working relationship, however, roles are formal and relationships function to further the goals of the business. If an employee critiques the work of a colleague who also happens to be a friend, it can create friction.

The researchers also found that workplaces with close ties among employees can inhibit knowledge sharing across the organization, as information travels through the bonds of social ties rather than through channels visible to everyone. Similarly, friend-filled workplaces can decrease the rigor with which teams deliberate on complex decisions, as friends are more likely to value peers' opinions rather than rigorous analysis.

A body of research from University of San Francisco psychologist Saera Khan found that in close-knit workplaces, employees are more likely to keep quiet about wrongdoing. In one study, inspired by the real-life scandal at the healthcare startup Theranos, researchers asked participants to imagine they worked at a biomedical startup where a colleague had exaggerated the product's effectiveness, and had no plans of stopping. The researchers varied their description of the scenario based on whether the company had a familial or professional atmosphere. Participants were less likely to report the wrongdoing if the workplace was more like a family.

"When you see a group as a coherent unit—which is what a family is—it's really very hard to break that unit, which is what you're doing when you disclose wrongdoing," Khan told me. "You are destroying the idea that this is a healthy, happy family that's doing well."

To be clear, friendship at work can provide undeniable benefits, but it's not uniformly positive. Rothbard and Pillemer recommend building guardrails for maintaining friendships at work, such as coming to a shared understanding about when to discuss nonwork topics and soliciting outside perspectives when making business decisions to avoid groupthink. In practice, however, the line between friend and colleague is hard to draw—especially at a company like Kickstarter, whose culture is rooted in fun and camaraderie.

Kickstarter employees saw both the benefits and the downsides of an extremely social culture. Employees regularly stayed late to catch a postwork concert at the office or attend an art show from one of the platform's creators. In the early days, there wasn't much of a divide between management and the rank-and-file employees. They all participated in the same game nights and went to the same happy hours. Sure, there was the occasional managerial misstep, like the time CEO Perry Chen hired actors dressed up as dinosaurs to wander around the office for a week in an attempt to infuse some quirkiness in the workplace. (Several employees walked out in protest.) But in general, Kickstarter continued to grow and the informal culture was an asset.

When business is going well, the consequences of a blurry line between work and play can be innocuous—such as an awkward hallway interaction or confusion about whether a postwork event is optional or mandatory. But when a business comes on hard times, social ties can fray in the face of mounting economic pressure.

"As humans, we don't want material relationships, we want social relationships," Taylor told me. "When the office presents itself as the arbiter and the origin of social relationships, we think 'don't look a gift horse in the mouth.' But then once things start to go wrong, the facade cracks." Because under the surface of friendship and camaraderie lies what really matters: money and power.

In mid-August 2018, the Kickstarter Trust and Safety team—which is responsible for maintaining civility on the platform—noticed users had flagged a project for promoting violence. This was relatively common; anyone with a Kickstarter account could flag a project for the Trust and Safety team to review. The project in question was called *Always Punch Nazis*, a tongue-in-cheek comic book about the United States' battle against racism, featuring a team of superheroes who, you guessed it, punch Nazis. The comic was clearly satirical, its pages bursting with all the over-the-top *pow*s and *fwoomp*s you might expect from a graphic novel.

At the time, the Kickstarter anti-violence policy stated that satirical violence that "punches up" at people in positions of power was acceptable, while violence that "punches down"—for example, someone in power targeting an oppressed group—was not. The Trust and Safety team ruled that the *Always Punch Nazis* project could stay up on the platform. Then *Breitbart*, a right-wing news site, ran a story calling Kickstarter out for leaving up a "violence-inciting project." The following week, Kickstarter management quietly overruled the Trust and Safety team's decision and ordered the project to be taken down.

The Trust and Safety team were experts on the policies that they themselves had crafted, and as the most diverse team at the company, paid particular attention to how policies might affect creators from marginalized groups. They wanted to know why the predominantly white management team had decided to take the project down. What policies did this project violate? Why did the company appear to be succumbing to pressure from *Breitbart*?

A senior member of the team asked her friend and colleague Amy out to coffee. She wanted to tell Amy about how management had overruled her team's decision. As a software engineer, Amy had relative job security in the tech-industry pecking order, so she pledged to try to do something about it. She brought the conversation out into the open, albeit circuitously, in the company's Slack.

On August 16, Amy shared a news article about another tech company, the payment processor Stripe, that had recently received backlash for processing payments for alt-right organizations. She wrote how proud she was to work for Kickstarter, a company that stands up for what it believes in. Though the post wasn't explicitly about *Always Punch Nazis*, Amy's goal was to start a larger conversation about Kickstarter's values.

Another engineering colleague echoed Amy's sentiments.

Then, without any prior coordination, Justine Lai, a member of the Trust and Safety team, chimed in. "Well, we're going to suspend the Always Punch Nazis project, so I don't know about that." This was the first time the rest of the company learned that leadership had suspended the *Always Punch Nazis* campaign. Justine's comment catalyzed what employees called a "Slack mob." Workers from across the company flooded the Slack with requests to see what policy management deemed the project violated. As comments and questions streamed in, the Kickstarter leadership team called an emergency company-wide meeting in the library.

At the meeting, the leadership team sat behind a wooden table that stretched the length of the room, while the entire staff sat on the floor beneath them like children. Though it was framed as a discussion, employees said it felt more like a courtroom. Never before had the divide between workers and management been so apparent. Flanked by Kickstarter's VP of community strategy and the director of the Trust and Safety team, Christopher Mitchell, Kickstarter's recently hired general counsel, spoke first. He made a brief statement that management had suspended the project for violating Kickstarter's policy on violence. Then the executives opened up the meeting to questions.

Many Kickstarter employees took the decision to take down the project personally. They had chosen to work at Kickstarter for its values-driven culture and were disheartened that management capitulated to the pressures of right-wing media, rather than uphold the policies Kickstarter employees had written. It

seemed hypocritical—especially from a public benefit corporation that loved to promote its mission of supporting artists.

Employee after employee took the mic at the meeting to
speak their minds. Brian Abelson, a software engineer, said management's decision was unconscionable and, if it were carried
through, he could not see himself continuing to work at the company. Camilla Zhang, the head of comics outreach—who was
regularly the public face of Kickstarter at comic conferences—
asked how management was going to protect her, an employee
who would come under fire from her community of artists and
writers if the project were taken down. Taylor, who at that point
had been working at Kickstarter for five years, made the case
that this was about doing the right thing and not some "legalis-
tic rendering of our internal rules."

"In that moment, it was just so crystal clear that it would be
unethical to let all the power in their organization remain in the
hands of those few people," Taylor later said. "They were not
responsible stewards of their power." The staff left the meeting
feeling angry and emboldened—angry at management's depar-
ture from the company's stated values and emboldened by their
fellow colleagues' bravery. Speaking up at the meeting was the
Kickstarter staff's first demonstration of collective action.

After he left the meeting, Taylor ran into Brian, the engineer who had threatened to quit, in the mailroom. Taylor looked
his colleague in the eye and shouted a single word: "Union!"

Historically, workers have formed unions to check managerial power. Collective bargaining can help workers ensure they get fair wages, benefits, safe working conditions, and a say in decisions that affect the entire organization. If familial workplaces are built on camaraderie and trust, unionized workplaces are built on contractual obligations. But in the United States, union membership has declined precipitously in the past few decades. At the height of organized labor in the 1950s, one in three American workers belonged to a union. In 2021, only one in ten did, the lowest rate on record.

There are various explanations for why union membership has declined. Legislation such as the Taft-Hartley Act and so-called right-to-work laws have increased the barriers to organizing and made it easier for companies to union bust. Occupations and industries where union participation has historically been highest, such as manufacturing, have shrunk, while job growth has been greatest in industries like tech, where unions haven't traditionally existed.

The day after the all-hands meeting, Cassandra Marketos, Kickstarter's VP of community strategy, sent an email to the entire company saying that leadership had reversed its decision to take down the *Always Punch Nazis* project. Employees swelled with pride, their collective complaints having paid off. But the following week, they learned the costs of their success.

Mitchell, the general counsel, came to the Trust and Safety team's next weekly meeting to send a message. "There's a huge difference between personal politics and company politics, and if you can't separate the two, you should find another job," he said, raising his voice. His tone played into one of the common tropes of mission-driven startups: either you put the company first or you show yourself the door. Will Pace, the director of Trust and Safety, told his team that he'd be setting up one-on-one meetings with each of them.

The following week, Justine Lai, the woman who first shared leadership's decision on Slack, met with Pace and Andrew Blancato, Kickstarter's head of HR. The three sat around a table in a windowless room. Justine was told that she could no longer be trusted and that she should think about signing a separation agreement. The next day, Justine was sent a separation agreement and termination package contingent on her resignation. She took the deal.

Justine's resignation lit a fuse inside Taylor. It was clear that this "family" was willing to part ways with one of its own over a Slack message. Executives spoke often about how everyone was on the same team. But when they forced Justine out, Taylor called bullshit. "They can fire us; we can't fire them," Taylor told me. "We were never on the same team."

The only way to rebalance the power, Taylor thought, was

for workers to organize. The day after Taylor learned Justine had been pushed out, he took out a pad of Post-its and scribbled down the names of coworkers he thought might be interested in a union drive. That week, he started making calls.

~~ℓ~~

As a hub of Kickstarter's social life, Taylor was well positioned to gauge workers' interest in organizing. The same social ties that made the company family-like also created the conditions whereby a union drive might be possible. After Justine's termination, rank-and-file workers began trading stories and noticing how what may have seemed like isolated incidents—inequitable pay and a lack of inclusive decision-making, for example—were actually part of systemic patterns.

Alongside Taylor, the other leaders of the organizing effort—like Travis Brace from the Community team, RV Dougherty from the Trust and Safety team, and Clarissa Redwine from the Creator Outreach team—weren't interested in organizing because they disliked Kickstarter. Quite the opposite. They organized because they believed Kickstarter and its employees were worth fighting for.

Clarissa remembers Taylor's call coming out of the blue. At the time, she was the company's lone West Coast employee, so the six p.m. call meant a late night at the office for Taylor. Taylor described to her the lack of input Kickstarter employees had in determining the direction of the company. He cited examples such as the *Always Punch Nazis* campaign and management's controversial decision to cancel Drip—another crowdfunding tool Taylor and others had spent the last year building out—before its planned launch. Then he got to the point. "Some of us have been talking about potentially forming a union," he said. "Would you like to join us?"

At first, Clarissa was hesitant. She genuinely loved her work, and was in the process of leaving behind everyone she knew in California and relocating her family to New York so she could be closer to Kickstarter HQ. She was intrigued by Taylor's pitch, but a union drive felt risky. She didn't want to jeopardize her livelihood at a time when she was about to uproot her life.

The hesitance to ruffle feathers was common among employees who considered joining the organizing effort. In tech workplaces, "there's such a family culture, and it feels very flat," Grace Reckers, an organizer with the Office and Professional Employees International Union, which eventually worked with Kickstarter employees on their union drive, told *Wired*. "There's this fear of conflict." But Reckers knows as well as anyone that emphasizing family-like company bonds ("We care about each other here!") is a common union-busting tactic. Employees need contractual protections, not corporate sweet nothings.

After sleeping on it, Clarissa recognized the benefits of unionization—for both current and future Kickstarter employees—

despite the risks. The next day, she let Taylor know she was enthusiastically in.

After she moved to New York, Clarissa, Taylor, and about a dozen other employees regularly gathered in Taylor's brick-walled podcasting studio around the corner from the office. The fridge was stocked with Sixpoint lager, and organizers took turns picking up pizza for the meetings. Organizing was exhilarating. "It felt like the Avengers," Taylor told me, with each employee bringing their unique superpower.

Over the next few months, the leaders of the union drive leveled up their organizing skills and recruited other employees to join the effort. RV taught the rest of the group some lessons they had learned from their past political organizing experience, and Travis helped lead new member outreach, but for the most part, everyone was an organizing novice. They spent early meetings Googling questions like, "How to start a union?"

One by one the organizers set up meetings with every nonmanagerial employee at the company to gauge their interest in joining the drive. These meetings took place during lunches and coffee breaks, breakfasts before work, and beers after, as it was important not to organize while workers were on the clock. Soon after joining the organizing effort, the others asked Clarissa to join its leadership committee, which raised her profile as a public face of the union drive. The lead organizers sent out emails to the entire company explaining the rationale behind the organizing effort, with their headshots at the bottom of each message.

As Clarissa began to become a more visible member of the drive, she started to receive pushback from coworkers who were less supportive of the union. This kind of policing among peers is common—both in union drives and in close-knit office cultures—according to various workplace experts with whom I spoke. "People become so passionate about the mission," Green, the *Ask a Manager* columnist, told me, "that they often act as if they are personally affronted when a peer who is not part of management tries to set boundaries on their time or what their labor is worth."

Not all employees were on board with the union drive. In an all-staff memo that was leaked to *Gizmodo*, three senior employees wrote, "Unions are historically intended to protect vulnerable members of society, and we feel the demographics of this union undermine this important function." They added that they were "concerned with the misappropriation of unions for use by privileged workers."

One time, after she was a known leader of the organizing effort, Clarissa recommended an idea for a piece of editorial content to a colleague on the marketing team, which was a regular practice for employees like Clarissa who interacted with Kickstarter creators on a regular basis. The colleague responded that Clarissa shouldn't tell her how to do her job and reported Clarissa's action to management.

Pushback came in other forms, too. In her first three years at the company—before she joined the organizing effort—Clarissa had received glowing performance reviews from her manager. But after becoming a more visible member of the drive, she started to receive "personality feedback," criticism, often gendered, that addresses a worker's character rather than their performance. She was told her "tone wasn't nice enough" and that she was "failing to build trust with management."

Taylor also began to receive more critical feedback after becoming a visible member of the organizing effort, but unlike Clarissa's, his feedback was based primarily on his output. He was put on a performance improvement plan and given specific metrics to hit if he wanted to remain in good standing with the company.

In the labor organizing world, this type of criticism of a worker's performance and character during a union drive is referred to as "pretext." It's a common union-busting tactic from management who might want to fire organizers but are prevented by law from doing so because of their organizing alone.

As Clarissa, Taylor, and other organizers met one-on-one with employees to listen to their grievances and attempt to stoke their interest in the union, Kickstarter executives became more vocal about their opposition. In a company-wide email, Aziz Hasan, who took over for Chen as CEO in 2019, declared that the company would not voluntarily recognize the union. In his words, a union would "significantly change the way we operate and work together," and the company would be "better set up to be successful without the framework of a union."

But the union effort continued to gain steam. In one-on-one meetings, organizers emphasized that they weren't just advocating for benefits and pay equity; they were also fighting for a say in the strategic decisions of the company. They were fighting for time-off increases commensurate with the overtime hours they worked and for protections in case their jobs were threatened. "I hope I don't need my seat belt," said Taylor, "but I'm still going to put it on every time I get in the car."

In September 2019, almost a year after Taylor first called Clarissa about unionizing, they were each brought into a conference room—the same windowless room in which Justine had been offered a termination agreement the year before—and unceremoniously fired with vague explanations. The previous two quarters had been Taylor's most productive quarters at Kickstarter, far exceeding every metric laid out for him in his performance improvement plan.

Clarissa and Taylor decided to forgo their severance pay, which would have required them to sign nondisparagement agreements, and both filed unfair firing claims with the National Labor Relations Board. "@kickstarter I will not be signing your termination agreement containing a non-disparagement clause,"

Clarissa tweeted on September 12, 2019. "You can keep my severance."

~⟡~

Requiring employees to sign nondisparagement and nondisclosure agreements is a common practice. It's also a way for companies to keep employees from surfacing wrongdoing. "There's no accountability without transparency," Ifeoma Ozoma, a former member of the policy teams at Facebook, Google, and Pinterest told me.

Ozoma helped pass the Silenced No More Act, a California law that allows workers to share information about discrimination or harassment even if NDAs were signed, after her own experience of discrimination at Pinterest. "People can't be transparent about what they've experienced and what might still be going on at a company if they legally can't talk about what happened." Ozoma believes that open communication is a prerequisite for addressing discrimination, harassment, and other abuses. "That doesn't mean that they'll be fixed necessarily," she said, "but there's no chance that they'll be fixed if people can't talk about them."

One major reason Taylor and Clarissa felt comfortable sharing their stories with me is because they chose not to sign NDAs when they were let go. After being fired, they each went public with their experience organizing at Kickstarter, which inspired widespread support from the general public for the Kickstarter employees continuing to organize. It also put pressure on Kickstarter management to curtail some of its anti-union practices. But nothing had been won. Before a union could officially form, it would first have to go to a vote.

In February 2020, five months after Taylor and Clarissa were fired, two dozen Kickstarter employees traveled from the Kickstarter office in Greenpoint to the National Labor Relations Board's downtown office to hear the results of the previous month's union vote. The vote had been nearly two years in the making. The organizers needed a majority of eligible employees to vote in favor of the union for it to be recognized.

"If you worshipped the concept of being boring, this is the church you would build," Taylor told me of the NLRB hearing room where the vote count took place. But despite the beige backdrop of government bureaucracy, the room that morning buzzed with a palpable energy. Taylor sat with RV and Travis in the back of the room. Current Kickstarter employees, representatives of Kickstarter management, and lawyers from the law firm the company had hired sat in rows ahead of them. An NLRB representative opened the sealed box of votes at the front of the room.

The representative read the votes, excruciatingly, one by one. Employees kept personal tallies, tightly gripped pencils slipping from their sweaty palms. After a half hour, the results were in: 46 yes, 37 no. Applause and tears filled the room. The Kickstarter union was the first to win wall-to-wall recognition at a tech company in U.S. history.

"It was like I had picked up an anvil when I first wrote out that list of names of potential organizers on the Post-its," Taylor told me. "And after that vote, I could finally put it down."

Before the end of the year, the vote paid dividends for workers. In May 2020, Kickstarter lost 39 percent of its employees to layoffs and company buyouts due to the economic strain of the pandemic. But rather than receive the two to three weeks of severance pay management originally proposed, the union negotiated for departing employees to receive four months' pay and a minimum of four months of health insurance.

In September 2020, the NLRB found that there was sufficient evidence that Kickstarter management had violated the National Labor Relations Act by firing Taylor. The following month, the company agreed to pay him $36,598.63 in back pay. The settlement was validating, but for Taylor the vote was the real victory.

"Power should not be concentrated in the hands of a few, period," he told me. "If you are under someone else's power, you should have a say in how that power is used. That's the world I believe in. That's the world I want to build. And anyone who claims those as their principles is commanded to organize their workplace today."

Professional relationships—at least relationships between managers and workers—will always fundamentally be about power, even at the most friendly, progressive, mission-driven workplaces. An empowered workplace, though, is one in which the terms of employment are clear and the power structures are not blurred by the rhetoric of "family."

In June 2022, two and a half years after Kickstarter workers went public with their intent to unionize, the Kickstarter union ratified its first-ever collective bargaining agreement with Kickstarter management. The agreement guarantees annual wage increases and pay equity reviews, limits the use of contract employees in favor of full-time jobs, and standardizes grievance and arbitration procedures, among other terms.

"When you're a worker in a system where you're only ever rewarded for outworking your peers, it can create a really unhealthy understanding of your place in the power structure," Clarissa told me. "We turned our friendships and shared experiences into power."

6

# Off the Clock

## On the myth that working more
## hours always leads to better work

*My father built a time machine and then he spent his whole life
trying to figure out how to use it to get more time. He spent all
the time he had with us thinking about how he wished he had
more time, if he could only have more time.*

CHARLES YU

osh Epperson is rolling a joint on a rock in the middle of the
James River in Richmond, Virginia. His long dreadlocks
weave together down his back into a loose braid. Two tins of
canned tuna, a plastic container of dried mango, and a lighter
sit by his bare feet. An Italian pilsner rests in the heel of his
left shoe.

"This is luxury," he says, as his hands spread wide to hold the
weight of the moment. Josh has an easy smile that often emerges
before he speaks, as if he's about to let you in on an inside joke.

Perhaps that's because thirty-eight-year-old Josh feels as if he is onto something others have yet to see. After more than a decade in the corporate world and seven rising through the ranks of a global brand consultancy, he has spent the last three years running what he calls "The Experiment."

The Experiment has three precepts. First, Josh accepts only work that he finds meaningful. Second, he accepts only work that pays well (his rate is $130 an hour). And third, he accepts only work that allows him to work less than twenty hours a week. Most weeks Josh works ten to fifteen hours, but his annual income hovers around six figures. Rather than leverage his expertise for more money, as is customary for most ambitious professionals, he's chosen to leverage his expertise for more time.

Josh's situation may seem anomalous today, but through a historical lens "retro-chic" might be a more apt description. For most of human history, the more wealth an individual accumulated, the less time they spent working. The reasoning is simple: when you've got money, you can afford to work less.

In most civilizations, leisure was a sign of status. The word itself derives from the Latin word "licere," or "to be permitted to abstain from occupation or service." Athenians thought leisure was "the highest value of life" and would devote entire days to creating art, playing sports, and contemplating the nature of existence. Aristotle believed leisure, not work, was "the goal of all human behavior, the end toward which all action is directed."

Somewhere along the way, Americans lost the script. Every

year, the average American works about six hours per week more than the average Frenchman, eight hours—a full workday—per week more than the average German, and three and a half hours more than the notoriously overworked Japanese.

It wasn't always like this. In the 1970s, the average worker in America, France, and Germany all worked for roughly the same number of hours each year, while Japanese workers consistently worked a bit more. Over the course of the twentieth century, organized labor and technological advancement drove down work time. But in the last fifty years, a strange trend has occurred: despite gains in wealth and productivity, many college-educated Americans—and especially college-educated men—have worked more than ever. Instead of trading wealth for leisure, American professionals began to trade leisure for more work.

For years, Josh exemplified this trend. He happily sacrificed more and more of his time for more and more income. That is, until one day in 2019, when he decided he'd had enough. He hasn't worked more than twenty hours a week since.

Josh's childhood was defined by "couldn'ts." The toys he couldn't buy, the clothes he couldn't wear, and, occasionally when the money was especially tight, the dinners he couldn't eat. He grew up with his mother and older sister in a Section 8 housing project in Reston, a northern Virginia town known for its parks, walking paths, and golf courses. But Josh knew a different side of the city. He remembers the flashing blue lights that flooded his childhood bedroom when police came to investigate a murder outside his window, the shade of the oak trees he rested beneath by the creek while he waited for his alcoholic mother to sober up, and the Nirvana albums that he spun on repeat in his Walkman. More than anything, he wanted to escape.

Josh found refuge in the counterculture: skateboarding, punk music, and pot. "I've looked side-eyed at society since I was twelve," Josh told me as we walked toward the river in Richmond, his home for the past two decades. "I knew there was no one coming to save me." Neither of his parents went to college. His dad came in and out of the picture, and his mom bounced between low-paid clerical jobs. So Josh always had a job, primarily as a lifeguard at the local pool. School took a back seat to work, skating, and getting high.

"Josh was a kind, curious, and adventurous kid," one of his childhood friends told me. "But skating just makes you rebellious; it's intrinsically anti-authority."

During his junior year of high school, Josh realized the majority of his friends would be moving away for college, and so he decided to turn his academic life around. He always had been an intellectually curious kid, but he recommitted to his studies with a newfound motivation: he wanted to make it out of Reston. Josh still remembers the bear hug he gave to his senior year algebra teacher after getting the passing grade he needed to graduate.

After high school, Josh attended Northern Virginia Community College for two years before transferring to Virginia Commonwealth University, which brought him to Richmond. He figured a college diploma might be useful down the line, though pursuing a career wasn't particularly important to him. For two years, he worked "as one of those people who waved the little glow sticks" for United Airlines at the Richmond airport. He worked five night shifts a week, from four p.m. until the last plane arrived after midnight. He was paid $10 an hour with no overtime, even when flights were delayed into the early morning. At the end of every shift, he switched on the flickering headlight of his bike and rode the thirty-five minutes home. *This is just not cutting it,* he thought.

Mainstream depictions of overwork often feature business executives checking emails on vacation or Silicon Valley entrepreneurs coding late into the night. In the U.S. at least, busyness is more often valorized than disparaged. The gig platform Fiverr, for example, ran a 2017 ad campaign praising those who "eat a coffee for lunch" and choose "sleep deprivation as their drug of choice."

It's important to recognize, though, that the reasons Americans work long hours vary widely based on industry and class. For every Ryan Burge, who works so much because of the meaning he derives from his jobs, or Fobazi Ettarh, who works so much because of her employers' outsized expectations, there is a twenty-four-year-old Josh: an exhausted employee who works long hours just to get by. According to a report from the Economic Policy Institute, the lowest-earning quintile of Americans worked nearly 25 percent more hours in 2016 than they did in 1979. As wages have stagnated for low-income Americans, they've had to work more hours to make ends meet.

Overwork is not simply a matter of the number of hours worked, but also the intensity and unpredictability of those hours. People in lower-paid jobs have less control over when, where, and how hard they work. At any moment, for instance, Derek DeRoche, a gig worker from Los Angeles, juggles requests from food-delivery, ride-hailing, and handyman platforms. When he's not actively on the job, he must spend time figuring out his next gig—time for which he does not get paid. "I had to be available a lot for it to be a serious source of income," he told me. "So much for being my own boss."

Additionally, as Silicon Valley gig-based platforms expand overseas, so do the American working standards of their part-time workforce. Even in countries like Norway and Germany that have strong labor laws, gig workers are often classified as self-employed workers, which precludes them from full-time employment rights, such as the right to paid time off or the collective bargaining power of a union. The toll of long hours that often goes hand in hand with low-paid work is exacerbated by fewer protections—both from the gig platforms and from the state.

At twenty-five, Josh decided to leave his job at the airport. He found an administrative job at a local hospital that paid $12 an hour. Though the pay increase wasn't life-changing, for the first time Josh was surrounded by people who were passionate about what they did. Josh organized the catered lunches during which doctors and residents discussed the most perplexing cases of the day, and he often stuck around to listen. "Being in the orbit of people who cared about how they spent their time to the point where they *wanted* to dedicate a ton of time to their job was novel," he told me. "It challenged my ideas about what work could be."

That said, medical residents might not be the ideal example of workers who *want* to work the hours they do. The medical residency model was invented by William Stewart Halsted, a surgeon who believed medical students ought to live at the hospital during their training to fully immerse themselves in their work. Halsted was also a notorious workaholic and cocaine addict. And yet, the tenets of Halsted's training model persist to this day. In many white-collar professions, long hours are the norm, and they continue to creep ever longer.

Take lawyers, for example. Most law firms have minimum

billable hour requirements for their employees. In big cities, average minimums hover around two thousand hours a year, which is the equivalent of forty client hours a week, but informal expectations are usually much higher. These billable hours do not include things like commuting, eating, non–client work, or, ironically, accounting for billable hours, which lawyers track in either fifteen- or six-minute increments.

Many law firms tie year-end bonuses to meeting certain hour thresholds. On one hand, this makes sense as many firms charge their clients by the hour. But according to several lawyers with whom I spoke, it also creates a perverse incentive that rewards working longer hours more than producing high-quality work. "I gain nothing monetarily from working efficiently," a litigation associate at a New York firm told me. "Instead, I just have to do even *more* work to ensure that I can clear my hours."

Of the many reasons Americans work so much, there is one constant that transcends industries: the culture of American management. And the culture of American management—one in which managers meticulously track workers' hours—is largely the legacy of one man: Frederick Winslow Taylor. Though Taylor died over a century ago, his *Principles of Scientific Management* remains one of the most influential business books to this day. If you want to understand how employers manage employees' time, you have to understand how Frederick Taylor looked at the clock.

Taylor may very well have emerged from the womb in a three-piece suit with a stopwatch in hand. Born in 1856 to rich Quaker parents in Philadelphia, he spent two years of his childhood traveling in Europe before attending Phillips Exeter Academy. Rather than become a lawyer like his Princeton-educated father, Taylor opted for a machinist apprenticeship at a pump manufacturing company. He then got a job at Midvale Steel, a successful steelmaker, where he quickly rose up the ranks. He was promoted from time clerk to machinist to machine shop foreman and, eventually, to chief engineer—all before he turned thirty.

At Midvale, Taylor started to develop his own theory of management. While working on the shop floor, he noticed his colleagues putting in minimal effort, which resulted in higher labor costs for the company. Taylor saw his colleagues' lack of hustle as a personal affront. As he advanced in leadership, he dedicated himself to figuring out how to squeeze the most work out of every worker.

Taylor used stopwatches on the factory floor to study the efficiency of both the machines and their operators. He broke down each job into discrete actions—pick up a piece of metal, place the metal on the lathe, mark where to cut—and then measured how long it took to complete each action. Taylor believed there was "one best way" to do every task, which revealed itself through close inspection. Every action was an opportunity to maximize efficiency, and thus save the firm money.

After twelve years at Midvale and a few years working for a large paper mill operator, Taylor opened up his own consulting business to bring his "Scientific Management" philosophy to the masses. Businesses hired Taylor to come in with his stopwatch, study their workers, and optimize their workflows. But there were a few problems with Taylor's "scientific" approach. He notoriously fudged the numbers, lied to clients, and inflated reports of his own success.

One client, Bethlehem Steel, fired Taylor after his recommendations did not actually yield any increases in profit. But that didn't stop Taylor from preaching his gospel to anyone who would listen. His skill as a writer and marketer trumped the unreliability of his data. He published multiple books and traveled around the country to broadcast his ideas. In Taylor's mind, workers were simply unintelligent cogs in the capitalist machine. He described the average steelworker as "so stupid and so phlegmatic that he more nearly resembles in his mental make-up the ox." Never mind workers' humanity; he saw their every action, their every second, as an opportunity to maximize corporate profits.

Taylor's Scientific Management approach still reverberates through much of the American economy, especially in the manufacturing and service sectors. And in an increasingly globalized world, Taylorism has been exported around the world. But instead of managers holding the stopwatches, today it's often faceless technology platforms cracking the digital whip.

Employees at Amazon fulfillment centers, for instance, carry handheld scanners with countdown timers that measure the speed with which they scan and sort packages. Uber drivers race a ticking clock to accept their next ride. At UnitedHealth Group, a multinational healthcare and insurance company, "low keyboard activity" can affect compensation and bonuses. And a host of startups with names like ActivTrak and Insightful now offer employee monitoring software as a service. Eight of the ten largest private U.S. employers track the productivity metrics of individual workers, according to a 2022 investigation by *The New York Times*.

"This type of work sets us up for the oncoming automation," DeRoche, the gig worker, told me when describing the endless orders that come through the food-delivery platforms for which he works. "We're just a little more robot-like."

In 2011, while working for the hospital, Josh started to explore his next career step. After years of working jobs that engaged only part of his brain, he knew he wanted to do something creative. Josh took a trip to New York City to attend a five-day conference called the Festival of Ideas. The conference featured keynote speeches from authors, pop-up meals from up-and-coming restaurateurs, and public art installations from the city's trendiest museums and galleries. Of the hundreds of exhibits, one project captured Josh's imagination.

The project was called FEAST, an acronym for Funding Emerging Art with Sustainable Tactics. At each FEAST event, a range of artists and organizations presented their project ideas to attendees. Afterward, attendees voted on their favorites, and ticket sales from the event were distributed as grants to the winners. *Brilliant,* thought Josh, *I've got to bring this to Richmond.*

After returning from New York, Josh and a friend got to work bringing a Virginia version of FEAST to life. Josh still worked at the hospital during the day, but his passion and attention lay elsewhere. The Festival of Ideas had sparked a new identity for him. Although his job title didn't necessarily back it up, Josh started to see himself as a creative.

"I was, like, 'Oh shit, these people [in New York] don't have a piece of paper that says they can be creative, either!'" he told me. So in the fall of 2011, Josh left the hospital job and began to flex his creative muscles. He wrote articles about gallery openings and concerts for local publications in Richmond. He produced the first FEAST Virginia event, which sold out. He began hanging out with more artists and entrepreneurs. Josh found his mojo.

After witnessing his community organizing skills on display at FEAST, a local consultancy hired Josh to plan a series of events to showcase Richmond's history. From there, Andy Stefanovich, a local marketing executive, recruited Josh to join his branding firm. At twenty-eight, ten years after barely graduating from high school, Josh began his first salaried job, making $45,000 a year. "The come-up from $12 an hour to $45k a year for me," Josh said with a smile. "I was, like, 'I'm fucking rich.'"

The firm was aptly named Prophet. And at Prophet, Josh was a star. In a sea of Ivy League and business school graduates, a community organizer who had taken a nontraditional path to the corporate world offered a fresh perspective. "You could tell when he first joined, he was very skeptical of the whole consulting culture and how much we worked," a former colleague told me. "But Josh adapted really quickly."

Prophet was different from any of Josh's previous employers. The office occupied the top two floors of a former grain sales building in downtown Richmond. Unlike the foldable cubicles at the hospital administration building, the Prophet office was outfitted with mid-century modern furniture and glass-walled conference rooms. Coworkers regularly went out drinking or played four-square on the office's second-floor four-square court. But in spite of the laid-back vibe, the work was intense. Prophet had a competitive, high-performing culture. "If you weren't getting promoted every two years, you weren't doing a good job," the former coworker said.

But Josh took to the fast-paced environment. Soon he was flying around the country to give presentations on social media strategies to life insurance companies and crafting "innovation roadmaps" for breath mint manufacturers. The agency became the center of Josh's life, social circle, and sense of purpose. "I believed I was on my path," he told me. "I wanted to be on the plane sitting next to the partner . . . I wanted to prove that I belonged."

As Josh shot up the ranks at Prophet, so did his income. He was promoted, and then promoted again. Soon he was making six figures, and his lifestyle adjusted to match. He bought flashy Daniel Wellington watches and sleek Nisolo leather boots. He moved to a swanky apartment in Richmond's hippest neighborhood and bought a shiny black Land Rover. He worked long hours and traveled for work multiple times a month. But even as the work wore him down, he interpreted his burnout as a sign of success. Busyness and purpose felt like one and the same. *When there are millions of dollars on the line, and the client needs it tomorrow, it's got to be good,* he thought.

The irony was that as Josh worked more hours, his work didn't necessarily get better. As he started to lead teams and take on more responsibility, meetings and corporate bureaucracy squeezed out the space in his days where he could synthesize what he had learned and generate new ideas. Still, Josh kept his head down. He was making $140,000 a year, an amount that was unfathomable to the young boy who grew up with a single mother in project housing. He was also vying for a promotion to become a creative director—a position he had coveted ever since he started at Prophet and had been assured he would get in the next promotion cycle.

One day, Josh's work mentor invited him to go for a walk in the company's parking lot. Josh knew what the invitation meant: He would finally gain the title to reflect the value he brought to the firm. He would finally be able to call himself a creative director. As the pair walked through the drab concrete lot, Josh's mentor turned to him and said, "I'm sorry, Josh, but you're not going to get it." Without skipping a beat, Josh said, "All right, I'm leaving." He turned around and walked the length of the parking lot alone.

The spell of work had broken.

"When I quit, it was not for time, it was not for a better living, a better pace of life, or work-life balance. It was because I was fucking moody," Josh said as we walked single file through a forest of oak and cypress trees. Josh turned his head back toward me every few steps as he spoke. "I thought I would just get a corporate job at another branding firm and apply for the creative director role," he said, pushing a fern to the side to let me pass. "But first, I knew I wanted a break."

After leaving the firm, Josh took some time to rest. He had earned it. For seven years he had worked in an office where employees regularly billed ten hours a day. For countless nights Josh had stayed up late with his team to "add words to little boxes in PowerPoint presentations." He had given a lot of himself to Prophet. He needed to reclaim who he was without it.

Josh decided to give himself a three-month sabbatical. For the first two weeks of not working, he knew what to expect. This was "vacation Josh." But after those first two weeks, he started to feel uncomfortable. "For the last seven years, I had interpreted that all the time in my day had to translate to economic value," he told me. "And so when I couldn't look back at my days and see an economic output, I started to feel like my days weren't valuable."

That feeling resonated. Walking with Josh, I thought about how I, too, had internalized Frederick Taylor's worldview. Consciously or not, I tried to optimize my every minute. Even as I chronicled the dangers of conflating our self-worth with our work for this book, I couldn't help but feel that days where I didn't add to my word count, interview a source, or edit a chapter were somehow wasted. I didn't need a bespectacled manager urging me to juice the economic value from every minute of my days. I micromanaged myself, using each checkout line and elevator ride as an opportunity to tap out one more email.

During his sabbatical, Josh had to actively resist the urge to move on to the next thing. He felt guilty for not *doing* more. But rather than avoid that feeling of guilt, he chose to interrogate it. "Do I believe that in our one short human life the thing that gives my life value is contributing to corporate work that has economic returns?" he asked himself. "No, my answer to that question is no."

Then, Josh asked himself how he *wanted* to feel. After days of waking up without a set agenda, walking on the same riverside trails on which we were currently walking, he stumbled upon an answer: "I wanted to be compelled by awe and wonder," he restated, as we weaved through the dappled brush. I might have smirked if not for the earnestness in his voice. "I wanted to steep myself in nature, and see how I fit into this world. That's how I wanted to spend my life," Josh said. "And that was totally contradictory to everything I had trained on professionally."

Still, Josh had no delusions about the capitalist society in which he lived. He needed to make money. But if he wanted to infuse more awe into his life when he returned to the working world, he knew he would need to make changes, including incorporating more unstructured time into his days. *Can I work only on projects I find meaningful, make good money, and work no more than twenty hours a week?* he wondered. It was certainly an experiment worth trying.

Josh began The Experiment by scaling back the obligations on his time and money. He stepped down from his role on the board of a Black film festival. He moved out of his swanky apartment to a cheaper part of Richmond and traded in his Land Rover for a Honda CR-V. Despite these downgrades, his new path also came with advantages. Josh prepared his meals and ate more healthily. He spent unhurried afternoons with friends in the garden. And he got back into regular meditation and exercise. "I could actually be well," he told me. "And the only way I could do it was by opening up more time."

Josh also saw how the added time benefited his professional life. He started working on projects for the Smithsonian and an urban farming nonprofit called Happily Natural. With more space around his work, his work got better. "In the old industrial model of employment, the more hours you put in, the more products come out," he explained. But if the product is an idea for a marketing campaign or a headline for a website, Josh found that there wasn't a linear relationship between how many hours he put in and the quality of the output. With more room to seek inspiration and iterate on his ideas, Josh was finally doing work that made him proud.

There's a growing body of research that proves how leisure and unstructured free time benefit creative work. Brain scans show that idle time and daydreaming create alpha waves that fuel creative insights and innovative breakthroughs. In one study, four days hiking in nature without access to technology increased participants' creative problem-solving ability by as much as 50 percent.

But Josh no longer simply treats leisure as grist for the mill. He doesn't unplug so that he can be more productive when he sits back down at his computer. Nor does he, like so many of us, exist in a perpetual state of half work, swiping down at dinner to see if any new emails have come in.

What surprised me most from my time with Josh was how active he was—writing on the giant butcher-paper scroll he keeps on the desk in his room, tending to the okra in the vegetable garden he shares with his three neighbors, attending gallery openings and open mic nights to support local artists. What other people might call "time off" is not a means to an end for Josh; it's an end in and of itself.

To be clear, not everyone can afford to take a sabbatical or to work fewer hours. Josh acknowledges that the money and skills he built up in the corporate world play an integral part in the success of his experiment. "This whole lifestyle that I've got going on would not be on offer ten years ago—I didn't have the skills," he told me. "Things have their time and things have their audience, but imagine if everyone who could were living like this? We'd change the economy."

Across the income spectrum and the globe, workers are running their own experiments to deprioritize work. Young workers in Japan, referred to as the hodo-hodo zoku, started a cultural movement to avoid promotions in order to minimize stress and maximize free time. In China, there's a growing social media trend of "tang ping"—workers "lying flat" to actively resist the expectation of constant work. Tricia Hersey, an American performance artist and self-proclaimed "Nap Bishop," preaches the gospel of rest as an act of resistance to capitalism through her writing and communal-napping installations. The r/antiwork subreddit, an online community of workers exploring less work-centric existences, has over 2 million members.

"Young people feel a kind of pressure that they cannot explain and they feel that promises were broken," Xiang Biao, a professor of social anthropology at Oxford, told *The New York Times*. "People realize that material betterment is no longer the single most important source of meaning in life." And it's not just young people asking themselves how a world with less work might look. Entire countries are asking this question, too.

When Iceland conducted two large-scale four-day-workweek trials from 2015 to 2019, there was no question whether the experiments would be popular with workers. *Less work for the same amount of pay? Sign me up.* The main question was whether it would fly with employers.

One of the main arguments against reduced employee work time is that it makes companies less competitive. Every minute you rest is a minute your competitors get ahead, or so the logic goes. But that belief is built on the faulty premise that there is a direct relationship between hours and output. A 2014 study of munition workers by Stanford economics professor John Pencavel found that productivity per hour sharply declined after working fifty hours. And Pencavel discovered that those who worked seventy hours didn't get any more done than those who worked fifty-six hours. The research proves a truth we know intuitively: more time to complete a task often means less efficient work.

Other high-profile four-day-workweek experiments have been run at companies like the social media startup Buffer in the U.S., the New Zealand–based estate planning company Perpetual Guardian, and Microsoft Japan. In all three cases, productivity increased as much as 40 percent with the decrease in employees' hours, while workers self-reported feeling less stressed and more satisfied.

What set the Icelandic studies apart, though, was their breadth. Combined, the two studies reduced hours from forty to thirty-five or thirty-six a week for more than 1 percent of the Icelandic workforce without reducing benefits or pay. The workers came from a wide range of industries and included teachers, police officers, construction workers, and employees in the Reykjavík mayor's office.

For context, Icelandic people work more hours on average than those in any other Nordic country. The country has a robust social safety net and low unemployment, but it lags behind its Scandinavian peers when it comes to productivity. "Worn down by long hours spent at work, the Icelandic workforce is often fatigued, which takes a toll on its productivity," the final report of the trials reads. "In a vicious circle, this lower productivity ends up necessitating longer working days to 'make up' the lost output, lowering 'per-hour productivity' even further."

Given this backdrop, the results of the four-day-workweek studies were staggering. Across industries, there was no decline in work output. The immigration department, for example, reported no delays in processing time. Other organizations actually improved their productivity. A government call center showed 10 percent *more* calls answered than a control workplace with longer hours. Workers reported having not just more time, but also more energy for hobbies, social lives, and family. And with well-rested employees, organizations maintained, if not improved, the quality of their services.

Perhaps the biggest barrier to systemic work time reform is simply employers' resistance to change, which is why studies like the ones in Iceland are so important. They proved with data that reforms like reduced work hours can boost employees' well-being *and increase* their output. Workers were literally able to get the same amount of work done in fewer hours.

However, while productivity-based arguments might help convince employers and legislatures to consider shorter workweeks, we shouldn't shorten work hours just because we can still produce the same amount of stuff. In addition to the business case, there's also the moral one. We shouldn't work less just because it allows us to be better workers. We should work less because it allows us to be better humans, not just better workers.

Yes, working less helps us be more productive. Yes, rest helps our brain function and improves our health, our mood, and our body's ability to heal. But in addition to all of that, more time away from work allows us to be better friends and neighbors. It allows us to pick up our kids from school and have dinner more often as a family. It allows us to exercise regularly and read for pleasure and create art that no one has to see. It allows us to find time to get involved in local politics and to take a nap when we're tired. Put simply, working less allows us to be fuller versions of ourselves.

"This [reduction in hours] shows increased respect for the individual," one participant in the Icelandic study said. "We are not just machines that just work . . . we are persons with desires and private lives, families and hobbies." Tell that to Frederick Winslow Taylor.

As Josh and I sat on the boulder in the middle of the James River, the sounds of chirping birds and rushing water in our ears, he told me to look around. "Do you see anything moving extremely fast?" he asked. An oak tree swayed in the wind. The river curved around a rock as if it were practicing tai chi. "In nature, it just doesn't happen," Josh continued. "Seeds have to sprout, then they have to blossom, then fruit, rot, and return to the soil before the cycle begins again . . . It takes time."

"Do you ever worry about how long you can keep this experiment up?" I asked.

Josh flashed his easy smile. "There have been times where the money has started to slow down and I ask myself: Is this working? Is this worth it?" He paused for a second as if his questions weren't rhetorical.

"But I hold. I'm not ready to walk out of the lab just yet."

# Work Hard, Go Home

## On the myth of cushy office perks

*The caveman was undoubtedly very pleased to find a good cave, but he also undoubtedly positioned himself at the entrance looking out. "Protect your back, but know what is going on outside" is a very good rule for survival. It is also a good survival rule for life in offices.*

ROBERT PROPST, INVENTOR OF THE CUBICLE

'm walking through a redwood grove with Brandon Sprague, a twenty-nine-year-old software engineer who looks like a young Dustin Hoffman if Hoffman let his hair grow long and spent his mornings doing deadlifts. Brandon is wearing an untucked blue button-down, gray chinos, and technicolored Converse, the design of which, he tells me, he wrote a bespoke algorithm to customize. Above us, a pink and purple sunset softens the northern California sky. To our left, bright red, yellow, and blue bikes lay strewn like forgotten toys. To our right, a crisp white sign pokes through the grass, its elementary school lettering unmistakable: *Welcome to Google.*

Brandon knows this walk well. For the six years he worked for the company, it was his daily commute—through the parking lot of Teslas and food trucks (vehicle charging and food are both free for employees), into the redwood grove, and past a fitness center, two gourmet cafés (*not* cafeterias), and a small babbling brook, before he arrived at his desk.

In the midst of it all, it's nearly impossible to tell where the campus begins and ends. We hear cheers from nearby soccer fields. "Technically, those belong to the city of Mountain View," Brandon tells me. "But I think Google paid for them." We pass an organic garden, a small waterfall, and a human-sized replica of the teardrop–shaped Google Maps icon. There are tennis courts, doctors' offices, and a restaurant that serves sushi on conveyor belts. *If I worked here,* I think, *I would never leave.*

"Though the outsides of the buildings stay the same," Brandon says, "they're always remodeling the insides to make them more Googley." I press my forehead to the glass of one of the offices to see what "Googley" might mean. A fake palm tree shades one of the desks, an inflatable beach ball sags on the floor of a carpeted hallway, and a graffiti mural of the word "wild" splashes across a wall. Because neither of us is a Googler, we can't go inside.

The need to keep the outside world locked out is understandable; tourists come from halfway around the world to take pictures of the Google campus's sculpture garden. But as we stroll past a cluster of Googlers illuminated by their laptops' glowing screens at seven p.m. on a Tuesday, I can't help but think that the locks go both ways.

Decades before Sergey Brin and Larry Page were born, authors like George Orwell and Aldous Huxley painted scenes of technology-driven dystopias in books like *1984* and *Brave New World.* "Orwell warns that we will be overcome by an externally imposed oppression," wrote media theorist Neil Postman. "But in Huxley's vision, no Big Brother is required to deprive people of their autonomy, maturity, and history. As he saw it, people will come to love their oppression, to adore the technologies that undo their capacities to think."

Walking around the campus reminded me of my own stint in the tech industry. Before I became a journalist, I worked at a startup with hot breakfast in the mornings and yoga in the evenings. I was #blessed with the perks of a venture capital–subsidized life. But I also think back to days when I was lured in before eight a.m. and stayed until well after sunset, like a driver on the highway who can't remember the last five miles of road. Life became work, and work became a series of rinse-and-repeat days that felt indistinguishable from one another. The ease with which I could extend the workday was not, in fact, a perk at all.

~~o~~

In 1903, the Larkin Soap Company, a mail-order soap business, hired a young Frank Lloyd Wright to design its "office of the future" in Buffalo, New York. As Nikil Saval describes in *Cubed: A Secret History of the Workplace*, the Larkin Administration Building's "concerted, unified conception of architecture, layout, design, and management seemed to anticipate and solve all the problems of management and office labor."

Wright's design offered Larkinites roof gardens, lunchrooms, bathhouses, a hospital clinic, a library, and a gym. The company held Friday night concerts and Sunday masses. Perhaps the office's most distinctive feature was its central courtyard. Natural light flooded the courtyard through large glass windows similar to a mall galleria. Early twentieth-century corporate buzzwords—"co-operation," "industry," "control"—were inscribed into the stone walls. In the courtyard sat the workers, "identically attired and coiffured women . . . guarded at the desk corners by four male executives."

Within this lush space, the line between progressive office design and paternalistic management blurred. Larkin created an environment whereby a worker's every need was taken care of, but also their every action could be supervised. In the context of turn-of-the-century labor movements, where unions and strikes threatened executive power, Larkin created a Taylorist work environment in service of what the firm called "industrial betterment." "What passed for workers' welfare could with a little imagination also be seen as social control," Saval writes. The Larkin Building was a harbinger of the sprawling Silicon Valley campuses to come.

The office itself is a technology, a tool that ideally helps people get work done. But like any piece of technology, how it's used matters far more than what it can do. The office can be a nexus of collaboration or a stage for corporate theater. It can be an oasis for deep work or a place where employees demonstrate to their managers how hard they *surely* must be working. Since the Googleplex opened in the early aughts, the company's Mountain View headquarters has been celebrated for its perks. Googlers play beach volleyball between meetings, book deskside massages, and sit down for multicourse dinners. But the true beneficiary of all the campus amenities is Google. They keep employees at work.

Beyond Silicon Valley, companies in other industries are calculating the return on investment of their employee benefits, too. As part of her PhD research at Princeton, for example, anthropologist Karen Ho spent a year working as an investment banker on Wall Street in the 1990s. While there, she found that two organizational "perks"—dinner and a free ride home—were central to the long hours synonymous with banking culture. If workers stayed at the office until seven p.m., they could order dinner on the company dime. "With no time to shop for groceries or cook, they soon become dependent on this service and even on the occasional day when they can leave before seven p.m., they stay in order to have dinner," she writes in *Liquidated: An Ethnography of Wall Street*. Then, if bankers reached the nine p.m. milestone, the company paid for their ride home. While complimentary dinners and rides home might keep bankers working late, another device, the BlackBerry, kept them "chained to the office while at home or 'on vacation,'" according to Ho.

Though BlackBerrys have since fallen by the wayside, the digital shackles persist. Workplace communication apps keep knowledge workers perpetually half-connected, in a state reminiscent of sharks sleeping with one eye open. "The modern knowledge worker is almost never more than a few minutes away from sending or receiving some sort of electronic communication," Cal Newport writes in *A World Without Email*. "To say we check email too often is an understatement; the reality is that we're using these tools constantly."

Ironically, at its San Francisco headquarters, the enterprise messaging company Slack has made an effort to discourage the phenomenon that its product helps perpetuate. Painted on the office wall is a message that summarizes the company's philosophy on work: *Work hard and go home.*

"There is no line you can draw between free kombucha and people's satisfaction in their job," Deano Roberts, Slack's former global facilities director, told me. "If the reason you're attracted to your employer is that they have free cupcakes, there are a bunch more cultural issues you have to unpack." The goal of the office, according to Roberts, should be to make it as easy as possible for employees to get their work done and then to get on with their lives.

Compared to the Googleplex, my walk through Slack's San Francisco headquarters was quite dull. There was no office gym, no life-sized Jenga blocks, no scooters buzzing down the hall. It felt like a place to, well, work. But shouldn't that be what offices are optimized for? The office doesn't need to be your bar or your gym or your go-to dinner spot—and not because cocktails or office gyms or catered dinners are inherently bad. It's because work should be a means to an end. And in the end, we should go home.

But for Brandon, my tour guide that evening in Mountain View, deciding when to leave the office wasn't much of a choice. That's because for the six years he worked for Google, Brandon lived in a ninety-six-square-foot box truck in the company parking lot.

Brandon Sprague grew up in a blue-collar family in eastern Massachusetts. His mom worked in an eye doctor's office, and his dad manufactured awnings. Brandon says his worldview is, in large part, a reaction to his parents. He describes his mom as a "stuff-a-holic," prone to impulse-buy items like a handheld massager or trinkets near the grocery store checkout counter. His dad is a "guys' guy" who rides motorcycles and ends his days at the bar.

Before Brandon left to attend college at UMass Amherst, he lived in five different homes. "I didn't really get attached to the idea of having a single significant space of my own to use as an anchor," he told me. Brandon has a young face with bright eyes but speaks with the steady confidence of someone who spends time considering what he has to say. Though he has a propensity to speak in tweets ("anything that's not sentient is a tool" . . . "money doesn't do a lot for you once you have enough of it"), everything he does—from the words he chooses to the brand of socks he buys—is intentional. After each question I asked him, he paused, as if to turn it over in his palm before responding.

To pay for college, Brandon worked thirty to forty hours each week for the Pioneer Valley Transit Authority, the organization that oversees public transit in a large part of southwestern Massachusetts. He started as a bus driver, but by the end of his four years there he had rewritten the software the organization used to manage payroll and routes. (Brandon taught himself to code at age thirteen.) After his junior year at UMass, he landed an internship at Google. Brandon didn't have a passport and had barely left his Massachusetts bubble, but at twenty-one, he moved across the country to spend the summer in California.

With its nap pods, volleyball courts, and on-campus dry cleaning, the Googleplex was no Pioneer Valley Transit Authority.

But what stood out most to Brandon was the exorbitant cost of Bay Area living. For his summer in Silicon Valley, he shared a two-bedroom apartment with three roommates. Each paid over $2,000 a month in rent. Brandon resented giving so much of his paycheck to a landlord. So, after he accepted a full-time job offer from Google the following year, he started to think about how to take advantage of the benefits of Bay Area living without incurring Bay Area costs.

In May 2015, Brandon moved to California with $22,434 in student loans, a few hundred dollars in his bank account, and a plan. He had two weeks until his first day as a full-time Googler, and he wouldn't get his relocation bonus until he received his first paycheck. Thankfully, Google had temporary on-campus housing for new employees (the GSuites, because of course) where Brandon crashed until work began. He took out a $9,500 loan from a local credit union and set his sights on finding a vehicle to call home.

When he arrived at Greenlight Motors, a used-car dealer specializing in cargo trucks, there weren't many options that fit Brandon's $10,000 budget. However, in the back of the lot sat an old white box truck with a faded orange Budget logo. One of the headlights was loose. There were cracks in the roof, and the floors needed resealing. But nevertheless, the truck piqued Brandon's interest.

He was reminded of his grandmother's house, where he had spent a lot of time as a kid. His grandmother had a set of old ceramic-handled silverware. One day, she noticed Brandon avoiding the spoons with cracked and chipped handles. "You know, Brandon, broken spoons need love, too," she said.

As he looked at that run-down sixteen-foot box truck, his grandma's adage came to mind. "I was, like, you know, I can love this truck, clean it up, and make repairs as necessary," he told me. He bought it on the spot.

Brandon spent his first day of full-time work and the subsequent half decade sleeping in the truck on or near the Google campus. Roughly a year in, the company caught wind that one of its employees—a software engineer making six figures, no less—was living in a box truck in the company parking lot, and forbade employees from sleeping in vehicles on campus. Brandon started parking across the street.

When it comes to delineating between work and life, not every worker has the same preferences. Nancy Rothbard, a management professor at Wharton, believes there are broadly two types of workers: "integrators," people who don't mind blurring the boundary between work and home, and "segmentors," people who have a strong desire to separate work from their personal life.

For one of Rothbard's studies, she spent time with a segmentor who worked as a firefighter. He had a set ritual for the end of each shift: change into flip-flops, drive home, and go straight to the bathroom. He had a rule never to bring his work boots into the house or to hug his kids until after he had taken a shower and changed his clothes. It was important for him to physically and symbolically shed his work life so that he could more fully participate in his life at home.

On the other end of the spectrum, there are people like Rothbard's Wharton colleague Adam Grant, who don't mind a more porous boundary between work and life. "Before I met my wife, my idea of a fun Saturday was working from seven a.m. to nine p.m.," he told Rothbard on his podcast. "The thought of leaving an email unanswered causes me physical pain."

Grant looks forward to work, which energizes rather than depletes him. "It's like saying, you know, 'I'm going to go to the movies and then I need to recover afterward,'" Grant jokes. "Why would you do that? You went to the movies because you were excited about it, it was fun."

Whether your work requires putting out physical or figurative fires, knowing your place on the integrator-segmentor spectrum might help you set healthy boundaries or articulate your preferences to your manager. For example, segmentors may prefer to stick to a predetermined schedule for working hours, while integrators might prefer to intersperse personal tasks, such as exercise or childcare, between periods of work.

Managers should take note as well, as the same policy might not be as effective for two different workers. An integrator might appreciate the freedom of a flexible deadline so they can accomplish the work on their own schedule, but the same flexibility might stress out a segmentor, who prefers clear timelines.

During Brandon's early years at Google, he was an integrator. There was little distinction between when he was on and off the clock. Every day, he woke up at dawn, worked out at the company gym, showered in the company bathroom, and ate his meals in the company cafés before he returned home to his truck. Almost all his friends were Googlers. He hosted a Truck-or-Treat Halloween party, where his coworkers came over to watch *Hocus Pocus* projected onto the truck's white walls. He did laundry in the same building where he worked, and inevitably found himself back at his desk between loads. On nights he didn't have plans, he hung around the office, coding until it was time to go to bed.

"It wasn't that my workload was too high, I just didn't know what else to do," he wrote on his personal blog at the time. But after six months living at the office, Brandon realized that he was spending 70 to 80 percent of his waking hours furthering Google's business goals. He realized that he had become a "zombie, constantly and mindlessly working away" at whatever problem he was given.

Brandon knew he needed to be more deliberate about when he was and wasn't working, so he decided to make some adjustments. He acknowledged that having the intention to work less wasn't enough. He had to actively carve out space for his nonwork self. He implemented a process to segment work from the rest of his life.

His first step was to set firm working hours. Brandon started working from eight to four each day. At four, he always changed physical locations—whether to another spot on campus, a nearby park, or a coffee shop in downtown Mountain View. Though he continued to eat the majority of his meals on campus, he made a point to never eat dinner at a café in the same building where he worked. For years, Brandon's new routines and boundaries worked relatively well. But the COVID-19 pandemic changed everything.

When Google shut down its offices in March 2020, Brandon effectively lost part of his home. He rented an Airbnb for a week, and then another one for two weeks before realizing that the gyms and cafés he relied on would not be reopening anytime soon. If he wanted to have a consistent place to shower, he needed an apartment of his own.

He kept his truck, but also rented a place on the California coast for a year, where he brought his living-at-work practices to his new working-from-home lifestyle. He continued to work consistent hours each day and only at his desk, which he didn't use for anything else. "When I'm working, I work there," he told me. "And when I'm not working, I am not there."

Brandon also decided to explicitly define the role he wanted work to occupy in his life. "For me, work has always been more of a tool, a means to an end," he told me. "Especially at Google, which has a very strong, active culture, you've got to make a decision on whether or not you want that culture to be your own internal culture as well."

For Brandon, the answer was no, which might seem odd for someone who used to literally wake up each morning at the office. But Brandon knew how easily the personal and the professional could overlap. Even subtle distinctions—referring to himself as, say, a person who worked at Google rather than "a Googler"—offered a semantic hierarchy that reinforced his control over work's role in his life.

For segmentors and integrators alike, the COVID-19 pandemic presented a host of new challenges. As the spatial and temporal separations between work and the rest of life disintegrated, knowledge workers were left to draw boundaries on their own. One study of over 3 million workers from the National Bureau of Economic Research found that working from home led to a 13 percent increase in the number of meetings and an 8 percent increase in the length of the workday—an average of more than forty-eight minutes per worker.

"The change in work schedule may be a consequence of a blurred distinction between work and personal life, in which it becomes easy to overwork due to the lack of clear delineation between the office and home," the researchers wrote. For many of those who were able to keep their jobs during this period of record levels of unemployment, the pandemic felt less like working from home and more like sleeping at the office. This was particularly true for people who worked from home while also raising kids, like Beverly Sotelo.

Beverly is an elementary school teacher from Oakland, California. She spent the pandemic teaching first grade from her 382-square-foot studio apartment while her five-year-old daughter, Cisa, attended remote kindergarten in the background. "I couldn't be a full-time parent because I had to be a teacher first," Beverly told me. But as a single mom, the pandemic forced her, like so many other parents, to try to be both.

Beverly set up her daughter on the floor of one side of the studio with a laptop propped up on a chair, and then taught her students on the other side while wearing headphones. Every hour or two, Beverly asked her first-graders to briefly draw by themselves, so she could turn off her camera and check on her daughter. At one point, Beverly set up a camping tent in the middle of the apartment so she could occasionally have a little space to herself. "It was hell," she told me. "I don't know what else to say."

Even before COVID, though, many offices were riddled with nearly as many distractions as a studio apartment with a cooped-up five-year-old. Open office floor plans, which have become ubiquitous in Silicon Valley and beyond, have largely failed to deliver on their promise of open communication and efficiency—the promise that "two workers from different departments or on different rungs of the ladder might run into each other by chance, and through the sheer friction of their sudden meeting, combust into a flaming innovation," as Saval describes in *Cubed*. Executives love to tout the "water cooler magic" of office life, but there's no evidence to support that working in person is essential for creativity or collaboration.

In fact, studies show that productivity and face-to-face communication actually decrease in open office plans. Employees report feeling the pressure to work longer hours and decreased levels of engagement. The open office "doubles as both a cost-cutting method and a way for everyone in the office to know what everyone else in the office is doing at a particular moment," writes Anne Helen Petersen. "Unlike the private offices that were once *de rigueur*, for most, open offices make actually completing work incredibly difficult, subject to constant interruptions or, if you put on headphones, suggestions that you're a cold bitch— *not much of a team player*."

When Brandon undid the Master lock and rolled up the overhead door to show me his abode on wheels, I was surprised by its minimalist interior. It was January 2022. For the majority of the past seven years, Brandon had called this hollow box home.

The inside of the truck looked like a 1980s interpretation of a futuristic prison cell. There were only two pieces of furniture—a metal cot from Amazon, topped with a twin foam mattress, and a tall black toolshed that served as a combined wardrobe, bookshelf, and medicine cabinet. Brandon kept about a week's worth of clothing, two Arc'teryx jackets, and a sequin mermaid costume for special occasions. The walls were covered with silver insulation panels, stuck together with royal blue painter's tape. "I never wanted the truck to be too nice," Brandon told me. "The point was to spend time outside."

Brandon had been spending more and more time outside. That's because a year prior, Brandon decided to leave Google. "You just get bored staring at the same four walls," he told me, without a hint of irony in his voice. In early 2021, Brandon joined an eight-person artificial intelligence startup. The office had no on-campus cafés or laundry rooms. "It's just a job," he said.

After the home tour, Brandon and I went to pick up his mail from a PO box he kept a short drive from Google's campus. The cab of the truck was spartan, save for a bubble wand that rested by the driver's seat so Brandon could blow bubbles while sitting in traffic. We drove south down Highway 101, past tech offices and Moffett Federal Airfield, where Google executives have special permission from NASA to park their private jets.

"I harbor an immense amount of guilt for all the good fortune I've had in my life," he told me over the clang of the metal door that separated the cab from the trailer. "I think guilt is a powerful motivator, so I'm going to use it."

Brandon hoped to channel some of his guilt into the next chapter of his career. Together with a former colleague from Google, he planned to move to southern Oregon to start a nonprofit. They named the organization Silicon Ally, with the goal of providing subsidized tech consulting to nonprofits that fight climate change and income inequality.

Without an employer to provide showers and meals, holding on to the truck made less sense. "The truck was a tool for doing a thing in my life," Brandon said matter-of-factly, as he changed lanes. "If I'm no longer doing that thing, the truck is no longer useful to me." The day before I came to visit, he had put the truck up for sale.

There's something refreshing about the clarity of Brandon's convictions. When I first reached out after stumbling upon his blog, I wasn't sure what to expect. I thought a software engineer who lived in a truck in his employer's parking lot might make for an interesting case study of the dangers of a life completely consumed by work. But Brandon's story was more nuanced. Whether or not you would make the same choices as Brandon, for those of us lucky enough to choose how work fits into our lives, the most important thing is that we actively make a choice. If we don't, work can expand like a gas and fill any available space.

From my desk in San Francisco, I certainly can't tell you what work-life arrangement will work best for you. Perhaps you're a segmentor, like Brandon, who needs firm boundaries to delineate when you do and don't work. Or maybe you're an integrator, who doesn't mind slipping in and out of work tasks fluidly throughout the day.

What I can tell you—and what became abundantly clear as I bounced along in the passenger seat of Brandon's truck—is that developing a healthier relationship to work starts with defining what you want that relationship to be. If not, your employer will happily define the relationship for you.

# The Status Game

## On the myth that status equals success

*When you get to my age, you'll really measure your success in life by how many of the people you want to have love you actually do love you.*

WARREN BUFFETT

For as long as he can remember, Khe Hy has seen the world as a series of games. As a nerdy, first-generation Cambodian American kid in New York City, the first game was to belong. In elementary school in the early 1990s, Khe was the kid with the funny name. He didn't have the money to buy the latest pair of Jordans, and when he was a teenager, his strict parents forbade him from dating. Instead, from an early age Khe turned his attention toward making money.

Khe's game plan was simple: if he earned enough money, he would gain status, and if he gained status, he would no longer feel like an outsider. He set his sights on college, where he planned to reinvent himself. In the meantime, he hustled. In middle school, Khe collected comic books and baseball cards—not because he liked them, but because he saw how they appreciated in value over time. By the fifth grade, he was already a regular at the StuyTown flea market, selling the cards for a profit.

In high school, Khe became fascinated with the potential of making money on the then-emergent internet. He knew that local businesses would soon need websites of their own. After teaching himself basic HTML, Khe pitched his services to his parents' friends, building websites for a travel agent and a florist, among others. At this point, Khe's life centered around two objectives: earning cash and getting into an elite college. He succeeded at both. While pursuing his side hustles, Khe graduated at the top of his high school class at the United Nations International School and was admitted to Yale.

In college, the games continued. Khe chose his major—computer science—because it had the highest average salary after graduation. He found a campus job at the reference desk in the library where he could "get paid to study." On the weekends, he worked as a mover to earn beer money. During his freshman year, he was already thinking about life after graduation. His goal was still to maximize his income, and the easiest way to do so at a school like Yale was to participate in a process called on-campus recruiting.

Very few bright-eyed high school seniors write their college admissions essays about their dreams of entering the worlds of finance and consulting, and yet those industries remain two of the most popular destinations for graduates of elite universities. One explanation for why: the companies come to the students, rather than the other way around. Every spring, dozens of employers descend onto the campus with briefcases and glossy pamphlets, eager to recruit the next crop of interns and junior analysts. Ambitious college students like Khe, with majors ranging from politics to poetry, trade their tank tops and sweatpants for blazers and pencil skirts in hopes of landing a position at one of the top firms.

As with elite universities, there is an understood ranking among the banks and consultancies. Goldman Sachs and McKinsey sit at the top, while companies like Bain, Morgan Stanley, and Boston Consulting Group also jockey for top talent. Company representatives wax poetic during information sessions about their unique culture and the transferable skills their interns acquire, but most students have few delusions about these firms' true appeal: the pay. This was especially true while Khe was looking for a job in the late 1990s, and Silicon Valley wasn't yet considered sexy.

Like many immigrants, Khe's parents instilled in him the value of hard work and a stable career. "We may not be the smartest, but we're the hardest working," his dad used to say. But growing up, Khe also saw how the stress of money weighed on his parents' lower-middle-class shoulders. After the family saved up for several months to buy a printer, young Khe watched a thief snatch the printer right out of his father's hands. They never got a new one.

As he looked toward graduation, there were only four jobs that mattered to Khe, which is to say there were only four jobs that paid enough: lawyer, banker, engineer, and doctor. Khe chose banking. He was still committed to his game plan: make money, acquire status, belong.

During Khe's recruitment process, the investment banks teased the glitz of the industry. They sent black cars to pick him up and treated Khe and his classmates to meals at the finest restaurants in New Haven. Young associates bought Khe $50 whiskey shots and rhapsodized about year-end bonuses and lavish client dinners. The career ladder in investment banking followed a clear progression, from intern to analyst to associate to VP to director. Khe could already see his path to the top.

For the first decade of his career as a banker, Khe swiftly rose through the ranks. He spent his college summers and postgrad years working on Wall Street, before he settled in at BlackRock, the largest asset management firm in the world. But despite all his professional success, Khe started to notice a nagging feeling that he wasn't playing the right game. He saw his superiors— the professionals in whose footsteps he would ostensibly follow— call into Saturday morning meetings while their kids played in the background. Khe regularly worked seventy-hour weeks, and he grew resentful of his colleagues who received slightly higher bonuses. The fancy dinners and new pairs of Jordans lost their sheen.

This uneasy feeling persisted like a pebble in Khe's shoe. But he ignored it, and set his sights on his next goal. He bought his first New York City apartment at twenty-eight. He was making a million dollars a year before he turned thirty. By thirty-one, he was promoted to be one of the youngest managing directors in the firm's history. There was always another promotion or end-of-year bonus that temporarily anesthetized his existential dread. But each time, Khe also developed a bit more immunity to these material accomplishments. "Success is like an addiction," Khe told me. "The first time you get high, you start hallucinating. But if you smoke every day, you need ten bong rips in the morning just to feel normal."

It all came to a head when, at thirty-three, Khe woke up one morning to go to the wedding of one of his best friends. His girlfriend noticed a chunk of his hair had fallen out, which he would later learn was due to stress-related alopecia. They had to leave for the wedding in a few hours. Frantically, Khe Googled short-term solutions. At a local Duane Reade, he found a bottle of alopecia concealer—essentially spray paint for hair—and used it to cover his exposed scalp. After the ceremony, Khe went to the bathroom and noticed in the mirror that the spray paint was dripping down his neck.

Here was a man who had achieved the highest levels of on-paper success. He was a high school valedictorian, Yale graduate, and one of the youngest managing directors in the history of the largest asset management firm in the world. And yet, he was so stressed that his hair was falling out. For fifteen years, Khe had assumed that one day his bank account would melt away all of his worries, but as he looked at his reflection—a thirty-three-year-old balding man, with specks of black paint splattered on his pressed white shirt—it was clear that all his wealth and status weren't going to save him.

When we say someone is successful, we rarely mean they are happy and healthy. We mean they make a lot of money. This is a truth Americans are hesitant to admit. When asked "How do you personally define success?" 97 percent of respondents in a 2019 survey agreed with the following statement: "A person is successful if they have followed their own interests and talents to become the best they can be at what they care about most." But when answering the question "How do you think *others* define success?" only 8 percent gave the same answer. Instead, 92 percent agreed that *others* would define a person as successful "if they are rich, have a high-profile career or are well-known." In other words, the majority of respondents believed that others define success based on status, fame, and wealth, but less than 10 percent admitted to holding that same view themselves.

Even if someone reports that their definition of success does not rely on wealth, fame, and status, it doesn't mean they act that way. Americans are largely driven by what writer David Brooks calls "résumé virtues"—the grades, job titles, and awards that might show up on your résumé. Résumé virtues represent a sort of external ambition, one that's validated by the gaze of others. And in the age of social media, each short bio and personal update is an opportunity to broadcast our accomplishments for others to see.

Khe's life was a picture of résumé virtues. He hustled his way from a lower-middle-class upbringing to the 1 percent. Khe's status, education, and finances represent the pinnacle of what our society deems successful. And yet he was miserable.

The status game that Khe was playing is the same game played among students who jockey for top grades, applicants who compete for prestigious jobs, and workers who vie for raises and promotions. It's a game that humans have played as long as they've gathered in groups, and yet it's also the cause of widespread suffering.

For our ancestors, status was a matter of survival. Higher status meant better access to food, mates, and safety. The same could be said today. People with high status have better luck on the dating market, better chances of getting a loan, and better access to healthcare. As Loretta Graziano Breuning writes in her book *Status Games: Why We Play and How to Stop*, "In the state of nature, social comparison has life-or-death consequences, so natural selection built a brain that responds to social comparisons with life-or-death brain chemistry." Our brains reward us with serotonin when we achieve higher status. But serotonin is released in short spurts and quickly metabolized. As the initial rush fades, we seek more and more.

While status can inspire excellence, it can also make us dependent on it. And the work of constantly jockeying for position can leave us anxious, stressed, and unfulfilled. This dynamic is particularly visible in the workplace, where employees' statuses are explicit. At work, salaries dictate our value. Job titles rank us relative to one another. The promise of promotions compels us to keep pushing forward. A problem occurs, however, when we enter into this game without first determining what we value beyond status. When our self-worth is tied solely to external rewards, we can spend our whole lives chasing carrots without ever feeling full.

"We seek status because we don't know our own preferences," Agnes Callard, a philosopher at the University of Chicago, told me. "When we don't trust our own definition of what is good, we let other people define it for us." Callard clarified that this isn't always a bad thing. Totems of status, like awards and recognition, can motivate us to achieve. But when we assume others' values as our own, we undermine our autonomy. Instead of determining our own definition of success, we buy one off the rack.

In certain scenarios, status seeking serves a clear purpose. Take video games. Most games establish a world with a clear goal and rankable achievements: Pac-Man must eat all the dots; Mario must save the princess. Video games offer what philosopher C. Thi Nguyen calls "a seductive level of value clarity." Get points, defeat the boss, win.

As Khe discovered, jobs like investment banking offer a similar level of value clarity. Success is measured by how much money you make—for the firm and for yourself. Promotions, bonuses, and raises mark the path to success like dots along the Pac-Man maze.

These metrics are seductive because of their simplicity. You might have a nuanced personal definition of success, Nguyen told me, "but once someone presents you with these simple quantified representations of a value—especially ones that are shared across a company—that clarity trumps your subtler values." In other words, it is easier to adopt the values of the game than to determine your own. Nguyen calls this phenomenon "value capture."

There are countless examples of value capture in daily life. You get a Fitbit because you want to improve your health but become obsessed with maximizing your steps. You become a professor in order to inspire students but become fixated on how often your research is cited. You join Twitter because you want to connect with others but become preoccupied by the virality of your content. Naturally, maximizing your steps or citations or retweets is good for the platforms on which these status games are played.

The *U.S. News & World Report* higher education rankings exemplify value capture at an institutional level. Before the *U.S. News & World Report*, standardized rankings for law schools didn't exist. Law schools each had their own missions and areas of expertise. Perhaps one school emphasized legal theory, while another prioritized corporate litigation. In order to pick a school, prospective students would determine what mattered to them, and then choose a school to fit their unique tastes. The *U.S. News & World Report* rankings changed that.

In a fourteen-year study, professors Wendy Nelson Espeland and Michael Sauder researched how the law school ranking system became an "engine of anxiety." In their report, they explained how universities reoriented their admissions standards and educational priorities based on the rankings, which emphasized GPAs, LSAT scores, and the employment rates of graduates. Schools largely did away with their varied specializations and missions in order to position themselves in a way that might help them rise in the rankings. Espeland and Sauder found that rankings dominated other factors in students' enrollment decisions. The "best" school in the rankings became synonymous with the best in the students' eyes.

The problem is not necessarily that *U.S. News & World Report* created a standard of excellence. It's that as students and institutions internalized the rankings as the standard, they no longer were forced to grapple with what they valued. When someone else determines what it means to be successful, there is no need to define it for yourself.

I felt this firsthand at an early crossroads in my career. After a half decade working in tech, I grew disillusioned with corporate presentations and marketing campaigns. I spent my days writing ads and PR pitches, but I wanted to be a *real* writer. So, I decided to pursue a degree to legitimize my intention. I applied to Columbia, Berkeley, and Stanford, some of the most prestigious journalism programs in the country.

Submitting the applications felt like making progress toward what I thought was my goal. There were boxes to check and essays to write. I was good at this game; I had spent my life jumping through academic hoops. Unlike law or medicine, though, a formal journalism degree is not a prerequisite for joining the field. Nevertheless, going to grad school was just something people in my family did. It wasn't until after I was admitted that I had to wrestle with whether I actually wanted to go.

I sought the advice of a mentor, the author Robin Sloan. We met for coffee on a drizzly morning at a café under an Oakland freeway overpass. After listening to me ramble on about the pro/con list I had sketched in my head, Robin asked me a question that cut through the noise: "If you could go, but you couldn't tell anyone that you went, would you still do it?"

I was so grateful for that question. For the first time, it made me consider my intrinsic motivation. Was I actually interested in learning, or just in being someone with a graduate degree? I decided to go, and I'm glad that I did. But if not for Robin's question, I may have never taken the time to ask what, irrespective of others' perceptions, mattered to me.

Public rankings and rewards can influence our behavior even before we enter elementary school. In one of the most famous psychology experiments on motivation, three researchers, Mark Lepper, David Greene, and Richard Nisbett, observed how students at a local preschool spent their free time. After identifying which kids often spent time drawing, they divided the young artists into three groups.

At the start of the experiment, the researchers showed one group of the students a "Good Player Award," a certificate with a gold star, red ribbon, and the student's name. They told the students in this group that if they drew, they would receive the award. Group two wasn't shown a reward, but if they chose to draw, they were given one at the end of the session. Group three was not shown or given any rewards.

Two weeks after the experiment, the researchers returned to the classroom to observe the students during free time. The students in groups two and three drew just as much after the experiment as they did before. But students in the first group—the students who had expected to receive an award after drawing—spent less time drawing than they did before the experiment. It wasn't the presence of the award but the expectation of receiving it that dampened the students' interest in drawing.

The ensuing paper, "Undermining Children's Intrinsic Interest with Extrinsic Reward," has become one of the most commonly cited studies to explain human motivation. Lepper, Greene, and Nisbett concluded that internal satisfaction from an activity may decrease when the promise of an external reward looms.

The researchers replicated the experiment several times with other groups of students and later with adults. Again, they saw that attaching a contingent reward to an activity transformed the activity from play to work. As Daniel Pink wrote in his bestselling 2009 book *Drive: The Surprising Truth about What Motivates Us*, "If-then rewards require people to forfeit some of their autonomy . . . and that can spring a hole in the bottom of their motivation bucket, draining an activity of its enjoyment."

When receiving an external reward hinges on your ability to perform in a certain way—whether it's reading for school or driving for work—it can change your relationship to the activity. It's something we know intuitively: working exclusively for external rewards rarely brings lasting fulfillment. As the old saying goes, *How much money is enough, Mr. Rockefeller? Just a little bit more.*

Khe's early life was dictated by "if-then" thinking. *If I get good grades, then I'll get into a good college. If I get into a good college, then I'll get a high-paying job. If I get a high-paying job, then I'll be able to afford fancy things. If I'm able to afford fancy things, then I'll be happy.* But as Khe got more of what he wanted, not only did the wins feel less meaningful, but his goalposts of desire kept moving.

Michael Norton, a professor at Harvard Business School, demonstrated this phenomenon in a study of more than two thousand millionaires. He asked the millionaires two simple questions: How happy are you on a scale of 1 to 10? And how much more money would you need to get to a 10 out of 10? Regardless of whether people had $1 million, $2 million, or $5 million, the respondents all answered the same way: that they'll be happier when they have two to three times more money than they have now.

The "if-then" trap commonly plagues elite athletes as well. After ten NBA seasons, eight All-Star selections, four scoring championships, and an MVP award, NBA legend Kevin Durant finally won his first NBA championship in 2017 with the Golden State Warriors. But the summer after, he became distant and despondent. Steve Nash, an adviser to the Warriors at the time, described it this way: "He was searching for what it all meant. He thought a championship would change everything and found out it doesn't. He was not fulfilled."

Michael Phelps, the most decorated Olympian of all time, described a similar feeling of emptiness after competing in his second Olympics. "It's like we dreamed the biggest dream we could possibly dream and we got there. What do we do now?" the swimmer told *The New York Times*. Phelps's ennui sent him into a spiral of substance abuse and depression.

Relying on external markers of success can leave ambitious professionals in any field feeling perpetually unfulfilled. This isn't to say that ambition and achievement are necessarily bad. But in order to satisfy our souls' deepest yearnings, there must be alignment between our values and the values of the games we play. We need to make sure our notions of success are truly our own.

Nguyen has a term for this process—value self-determination—which he considers the antidote to value capture. Value self-determination is simply figuring out what you care about for yourself. Figuring out your values allows you to tailor your definition of success to your unique personality and life circumstances. After finishing a video game, a player may take a step back to ask whether the game was worth it, whether the game was a good use of their time. But in careers, there are fewer built-in pauses. This was certainly true for Khe. It took a series of changes in his life for him to realize that the values by which he was living were not actually his own.

One afternoon, one of Khe's direct reports at BlackRock asked for advice on whether or not to attend business school. For someone looking to move up in the finance world, an MBA credential can be worthwhile. Khe thought business school might allow his mentee to round out his education and take a break from the grind of Wall Street, so he advised him to give it a shot. The mentee listened to Khe's advice and chose to go.

When one of Khe's bosses found out, however, he was furious. "He was one of our top performers," Khe's boss shouted. "I can't believe you let him leave us." Khe knew why he had joined the finance world: to make money. But in that conversation with his boss, he was forced to confront how the firm's values diverged from his own. The company cared about its employees' well-being only insofar as it benefited the company.

Then, in 2014, Khe's wife gave birth to their first daughter, Soriya. When Khe told his closest confidants that he was unhappy and considering leaving BlackRock, they'd say things like "That's so risky" or "What about your daughter?" But thinking about his newborn daughter was an inspiration, not a deterrent, for Khe to ultimately leave the job he had grown to dread.

Fatherhood put Khe's life in perspective. "I realized the riskier thing is my kid watching their dad be checked out and doing something just for money," he told me. Hitting his year-end bonus was no longer his North Star. Becoming a parent inspired him to change course.

In 2015, Khe left BlackRock. Again, his bosses were dumbfounded. At BlackRock, Khe had job security, a seven-figure annual income, and a fancy job title. But his superiors couldn't see that Khe had lost his enthusiasm to play the finance game. He was thirty-five years old, with a toddler, a partner who'd recently graduated from an MFA program in painting, and no next job lined up.

Soon after the initial rush from leaving the finance world behind, the questions began. His friends and former colleagues asked, "What's next?" All it took was one parent at Soriya's day care to ask "What do you do?" to send Khe into a spiral of dread.

Games tell us exactly what we should be doing, and exactly how well we're doing it. They provide a sort of existential balm. So it makes sense that within months of leaving BlackRock, Khe was looking for a new game to play. He thought about joining a tech company. He dabbled with life coaching. He briefly entertained the idea of starting a venture capital firm. But all of these avenues felt like doing the same work in different clothes. They were still games that Khe was interested in for the status he might accrue rather than the joy of the work itself. But there was one activity, Khe soon realized, that made him feel like time was melting away.

In his newfound free time, Khe filled his days with podcasts, magazine articles, and YouTube videos. He was stumbling on so much inspiring content that he decided to send an email with recommendations to a group of thirty-six friends. Khe felt like a high schooler making a mixtape—delighted to curate something for others to enjoy. The subject line read: "Some Rad Reads from my Recent Vacation." The email itself contained four article links, two YouTube videos, and a podcast episode. The earnest last line read "Not sure when I'll find the time for the next one."

The email struck a nerve. Nearly every recipient replied with how much they appreciated the recommendations. Some friends even forwarded it to others. This signaled to Khe that he was onto something. He sent out more recommendation emails, and his recipient list kept growing. Eventually he decided to name the newsletter *RadReads*. *RadReads* became the basis for Khe's next act.

Today the newsletter has more than forty thousand subscribers. Khe and his family moved from Manhattan to Manhattan Beach, California. Khe earns a living through *RadReads* and an online course he created called "Supercharge Your Productivity," which helps "highly-skilled professionals get more done without working longer hours or hacking together tools."

Khe acknowledges the irony of leaving the grind of Wall Street only to teach others how to be productive. But in his mind, the productivity course functions like a Trojan horse; its true purpose is to help his students build lives more closely aligned with their values. Lessons on "reframing non-productive moments," "tending to the important but not urgent parts of life," and "learning how to relax" are interspersed between modules on productivity research and task management strategies. Ultimately, Khe hopes to teach students to live life on their own terms, which his new lifestyle has certainly afforded him. He surfs every day, never misses a family dinner, and always puts his daughters—he now has two—to bed. "Even if I sold *RadReads* for a couple of million dollars," he told me, "it would do nothing to change my happiness."

I recently took a trip down to southern California to see the new life Khe had created for himself. It was a Friday afternoon. Against a seventy-four-degree cloudless sky, the palm trees lining the street looked as if they were posing for a postcard. Khe answered the door in his standard cool-dad getup: blue Air Max sneakers, tapered sweatpants, and a gray V-neck T-shirt.

On the shelf in his office sat a stack of books that neatly summed up his new lifestyle: *The Artist's Way* by Julia Cameron, *Surf Is Where You Find It* by Gerry Lopez, and *Range* by David Epstein. Two surfboards leaned on the wall, framing the background of where he takes his Zoom calls. Next to the boards hung a black-and-orange pennant that read "Dumbo, NYC," an homage to a previous life.

Khe described his daily routine to me: he meditates every morning, walks one block to drop his daughters off at school, and then heads to the Pacific Ocean, which he affectionately calls "the board room" despite his wife's eye rolls.

Khe's new life is still marked by the status game. The surfboards in his office are their own type of public statement aimed at soliciting others' approval. The ability to go to the beach in the middle of the day—and tell people about it—is a kind of flex. But the difference is that now Khe is playing a game he actually enjoys playing.

The skeptic in me believes that the lifestyle Khe created was possible only because of the years he spent on Wall Street. Sure, he sacrificed his future earning potential, but he had already "made it." He'd already accrued the résumé virtues. His substantial nest egg lessened the risk of changing course to pursue a more values-aligned path. But as I sat with Khe in his garage, wet suit and old-school hip-hop posters hanging on the wall, his wife painting in the corner, and Soriya drawing rainbows in sherbet chalk on the sidewalk, I realized that the peace Khe feels is not because he ignores what others value. It's because he's balanced what others value with what he values himself.

Choosing a career based solely on one's desires without considering what the market values can, for example, lead people to assume great amounts of debt for schooling that might not lead to practical job prospects. It can lead to situations in which artists can't focus on their art because they live in a constant state of anxiety about how they'll make rent. But alternatively, a career choice solely based on the demands of the market, without considering the demands of one's heart, can lead to situations in which people spend their lives climbing ladders they never wanted to be on in the first place. Even if you *are* passionate about what you do, the urge to climb the career ladder's endless rungs can taint the intrinsic rewards of what drew you to a particular line of work in the first place.

The key is to craft a personal definition of success that takes into account what you value *and* what the market values—in the words of theologian Frederick Buechner, to figure out "where your deep gladness and the world's deep hunger meet." Certainly, Khe's financial situation helped him design a beautiful life, but there's another ingredient that contributes to his peace of mind—the lack of which keeps some of the richest Wall Street bankers from ever feeling fulfilled. Khe has cultivated an appetite for what he already has. He understands his personal definition of good enough.

What stood out from my visit to Khe's California home wasn't the sunshine or the waves or any of the other trappings of a man in his midforties who had seemingly found his version of bliss. It was the timbre of his voice—the Sunday morning pace with which he talked, as if he couldn't remember the last time he had to hurry. There were no more games to win.

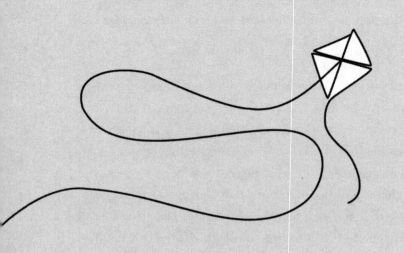

# A World with Less Work

## On the myth of personal boundaries

> *People tend to personalize what is a societal issue:* they *chose the wrong job or* they *chose the wrong partner or* they *didn't save enough money. A lot of times, we are working within this system that limits what choices we have.*
>
> TARA JEFFERSON

On the day after Thanksgiving, I find myself in a familiar situation: working on a holiday. The irony is not lost on me. Here I am, working on a book about the culture of overwork in America on a day that I'm being paid to rest. My morning was not very productive, which I could have anticipated given the wine and mounds of beige-colored foods I consumed the night before. But I still judge myself for not being as productive as I think I should be, and for working on my day off, which, by my own twisted logic, will probably drive me to work even longer.

The truth is, I'm embarrassed by how my sense of self-worth

is tethered to my productivity. Despite writing a book about right-sizing work's place in our lives, I'd be lying if I told you I'd found an easy way to do so myself. For starters, I'm writing this book on the side of my full-time job. I've spent the past few months working fifty to sixty hours a week to get it done. I'm proud after the weeks that I hit my writing goal and ashamed after the weeks that I don't.

Without my realizing it, working on this book has become central to my identity. I'm still playing with the mouthfeel of calling myself an author, but like a Harvard graduate and his alma mater, I need little prompting to bring the book up in casual conversation. I wear it like an enamel pin on my jacket.

And then there's the fact that despite writing about the dangers of expecting work to always be a source of fulfillment, most of the time I really do love what I do for a living. I feel incredibly lucky to have found a job in design that challenges me, ignites my creativity, and still allows me to do what I'm passionate about—reporting and writing—when I'm not on the clock.

When I started this project, I was motivated by two personal questions: How did my job become so central to my identity? And how might I separate my self-worth from my output? Two years later, I have no simple answers. But I don't think that's a failure of my reporting. Rather, I think, it's the result.

If I learned anything from the dozens of people I spoke to for this book, it's that negotiating our relationship to work is complex. At various moments, I identified with each person I interviewed—with Divya's unfettered ambition that drove her to burnout, with Fobazi's idealization of and subsequent disillusionment with her dream job, with Megan's listlessness, and with Khe's desire to quit it all and start again.

So, even though we've reached the "what can we do about it?" part of the book, I'm wary of offering any quick fixes to address our fraught relationship to work. Although you may be craving an easy way to develop a healthier relationship with your job, I'm afraid there is no ten-step plan. That's because there is no universal answer to the question of what role work ought to play in our lives. Our relationship to work is not fixed, nor should we want it to be. It's by wrestling with work's place that we uncover what we care about.

One of the main issues with overwork is that many of us have internalized the hustle culture that surrounds us. While I was writing this book, there was no boss mandating when I should or shouldn't work. I told myself that I wasn't going to let the writing process take over my life, that I would build periods of rest into my weeks. But despite all that, I still teetered on the edge of burnout. The problem with self-imposed boundaries is that they're permeable. It was too easy to let my fear of not finishing the manuscript on time or the feeling that I didn't *deserve* a break stop me from honoring my intentions.

In the words of author James Clear, "It's hard to change your habits if you never change the underlying beliefs that led to your past behavior." As long as I believed that my self-worth was contingent on my ability to produce, the drive to produce more would always trump my intention to work less.

Furthermore, overwork is a systemic issue—one that is the result of economic, political, and cultural factors—and thus there are limits to individual interventions. All too often, the onus to carve out and protect space for our nonwork selves falls on workers. Common antiburnout advice like "set a boundary" or "practice self-care" crumbles without institutional support behind it. If your company is understaffed, or it's the end of a quarter, or your pay is tied to your hours, setting a personal boundary is like trying to shield yourself from the sun with a cocktail umbrella.

Put simply, the problem with personal boundaries is that they inevitably break. "When cultivating a healthy working culture becomes the responsibility of the individual, it will always fail. Full stop," writes Anne Helen Petersen. "The responsibility for better culture lies with the workplace itself—which [is] uniquely equipped to construct the sort of guardrails that can actually protect employees, particularly those early in their career and frantic to distinguish themselves, from the freight train of work."

But there are limits to structural interventions, too. At the organization level, generous vacation policies and wellness benefits without a reduction in the amount of work managers expect from workers do little to change the culture. As Khe told me, after fifteen grueling years on Wall Street, a two-week vacation was not going to magically resurrect him.

At the policy level, too, governmental protections make a meaningful impact only when they have real consequences. France, for example, is often heralded for its "Right to Disconnect" legislation that, as of 2017, requires companies with at least fifty employees to limit calls and emails after hours. But results have been modest. One research study found that 97 percent of survey participants have not seen any meaningful change since the law was introduced. "Let's not delude ourselves," one French HR manager said. "Even on holidays in this company, managers are always, always connected."

Similarly, on the other side of the globe Japan leads the world with its paternity leave policy: fathers are given up to a year of paid leave. But there's a chasm between policy and practice. In 2017, a paltry 5 percent of fathers took the paid leave to which they were entitled. This highlights two prerequisites for creating a healthier relationship to work: (1) the structural protections to ensure employees can have a life outside of work; and (2) the cultural will to do so.

Changing the culture of work will require more than companies declaring mental health holidays or workers taking up hobbies. For many of us, it will require a fundamental reimagining of work's role in our lives. Institutions will have to change how they operate, and workers will have to unlearn the belief that they are only as valuable as what they produce. You may kindly line up behind me.

All this said, I still have hope. Amid all the fear and suffering of the COVID-19 pandemic, actions taken in the months after March 2020 proved that change is possible. Policies like guaranteed income and universal childcare assistance, once thought to be progressive pipe dreams, became realities, albeit temporarily. Organizations that had previously deemed remote work to be unfeasible adapted to more flexible ways of working. Individuals whose lives revolved around their workplace were forced to reckon with who they were when they weren't at the office. And workers who felt underpaid, underprotected, and underappreciated quit at unprecedented rates. The pandemic spurred not only the Great Resignation but also a Great Reconsideration. It showed us that our standard ways of working can shift, which makes me cautiously optimistic for the future.

The activist Dana White recently posed a simple question on Twitter: "If capitalism wasn't a thing and you had all your needs met, what would you do with your life?" Ten thousand people's replies paint a picture of a world without work as the gravitational center around which the rest of life orbits.

People wrote that they would become amateur astronomers, urban gardeners, sidewalk poets, and social workers. Perhaps my favorite response was: I'd keep doing exactly what I'm doing with less worry, frustration, and trauma about the money. It's notable that people's visions didn't exclude labor. But removing it as a prerequisite for survival expanded how they conceived of what's possible.

It's with that spirit of possibility that I offer a few provocations for how we might decenter work in our lives. The first one is for governments, the second one is for companies, and the last one is for you.

## 1 • DISENTANGLE SURVIVAL AND EMPLOYMENT

I was recently interviewing Adam Haar Horowitz, a researcher at MIT who studies sleep and dreams, when he asked me to try an experiment. "Picture yourself trying to fall asleep in a hotel room," he said. *Easy enough,* I thought. "Okay, now picture yourself trying to fall asleep in a hotel room with the door wide open." Immediately, my entire body tensed. There was certainly no way I could fall asleep when a deranged clown might walk in at any moment.

In order to rest and, by extension, to dream, we first need to feel safe. If we don't, our mammalian minds will keep part of our brains alert to scan for threats.

I think a similar biological force drives my tendency to overwork. Despite my gainful employment and the support systems around me, I still fear, however irrationally, that I'll lose my livelihood—or at least lose my career momentum. Unless I over-deliver, my logic goes, unless I continually prove my worthiness, I will somehow fall behind. I've adopted the values of capitalism as my own: Growth is progress. Stagnation is death.

Across the country, researchers are studying how to best address the economic realities and fundamental needs that keep so many Americans from resting easy. Warning: I'm about to talk about universal basic income, which has become a cliché in work-related books. Personally, I'm less interested in guaranteed income as a policy than as a moral stance—one that treats our basic human needs as basic human rights, rather than as benefits we must earn via paid employment.

In practice, the reknitting of our frayed social safety net could take many forms. It could mean shedding our embarrassing status as the only developed nation without federally mandated paid leave. It could mean forgiving the anvil of student debt that still weighs on the shoulders of tens of millions of Americans. It could mean expanding the Child Tax Credit, which has been proven to be an effective lever to alleviate poverty. Or it could mean reimagining our broken healthcare system, on which the United States spends a whopping *42 percent* more per capita than any other country in the world.

Instead, I use UBI as an example because it illustrates the cascade of good—for workers and our economy—that can result from raising the economic baseline for everyone. In a country with such high healthcare, education, and childcare costs, even college-educated professionals are not immune to the pangs of economic uncertainty.

As a reference point, for two years the city of Stockton, California, ran an experiment in which it gave 125 residents a $500 no-strings-attached monthly stipend. There were no work requirements or limits on how the residents could spend the money. Nearly 40 percent of the participants spent their stipends on food. Others used the money to send their kids to football camp and to replace the gaskets on their cars. Forty-eight-year-old Zohna Everett gave $50 every month to her church and then spent the rest on DirecTV, utility bills, car insurance, rent, and date nights with her husband.

The stipend also afforded Zohna the stability to secure a full-time job. After losing her job as a Department of Defense logistics specialist in 2018, she had been working gigs for DoorDash and Uber while taking college classes online. But over the course of the trial, she landed a job at the nearby Tesla plant. "I can breathe, you know?" she said, reflecting on the impact of additional cash.

Zohna's move into full-time employment contradicts some of the common critiques of UBI and the expansion of social services. Her newfound economic stability increased rather than decreased her pursuit of full-time work. In fact, Stockton residents who received the stipend were 12 percent *more* likely to have a full-time job after the experiment. Recipients of the stipend also reported feeling lower levels of anxiety and depression than their control-group counterparts.

But perhaps the most encouraging finding of the Stockton UBI trial was that the added money created "new opportunities for self-determination, choice, goal-setting, and risk-taking" for residents. In short, it gave participants more agency. Some, like Zohna, chose to find more stable work. Others chose to invest in their family or in their community. Natalie Foster, president of the Economic Security Project, the nonprofit that ran the UBI experiment, told me that "the Stockton trial did not reify an innate human need to work." Rather, she saw the trial as an example of what happens when workers gain more *choice* in their work.

To me, what stands out from the Stockton trial is the same thing that stands out from the Great Resignation data: a modicum of a safety net is all it takes for workers to leave jobs that are not good enough. A Pew Research survey found that the three most common reasons workers quit in 2021 were low pay (63 percent), no opportunities for advancement (63 percent), and feeling disrespected at work (57 percent). But the majority of the nearly 50 million Americans who quit their jobs in 2021 did not stay out of the workforce. They found better jobs—jobs with better pay, more flexible hours, and better benefits. And those who left the workforce altogether—to retire, care for loved ones, or take a break—are no less dignified for doing so.

American politicians often talk about full-time work as if it were a precondition for dignity. It's the same ethos behind policies that require people to be employed in order to receive welfare benefits. And although I agree that work can give people a sense of independence and purpose, paid labor is not the only means to that end. There are millions of parents and caregivers whose work is no less dignified because it is unpaid. There are millions of Americans who lost their jobs during the pandemic who are no less worthy of respect because they were let go—often through no fault of their own.

To decouple our human needs from our employment status is to declare that each of us has worth whether or not we have a full-time job. It creates a foundation upon which we can think more expansively about what it means to do good work, but also what it means to live a good life. It allows us to rest without the door wide open.

## 2 • SHOW, DON'T TELL

In 1996, Steelcase, one of the world's leading furniture manufacturers, installed a strange piece of art in its New York City office: a six-by-four-foot glass case that housed 1,500 ants. The installation was meant to be a rallying cry for an exciting new age in which the lines between work and life blur.

"Work is dramatically different than it used to be," Dave

Lathrop, a Steelcase manager, said. "For more people, work and nonwork are blending. Ants live to work, and work to live." But as *The Wall Street Journal* noted at the time, harvester ants typically live for only three to four months. A more apt interpretation might have been, "You work, and then you die."

Harvester ants scuttling around inside a glass case is a suitable symbol for the state of work in America today. A 2021 survey from the Society for Human Resource Management found that 41 percent of Americans feel burned out. Only 36 percent of employees feel engaged at work. Another study, this one from McKinsey, found that two out of every five workers were planning to leave their job in the next three to six months. Notably, 47.8 million Americans actually did quit their jobs in 2021, the highest number ever recorded. Similar trends occurred in countries around the world.

Clearly, high levels of burnout and disengagement are systemic issues that meditation apps and Zoom happy hours won't cure. And employers are starting to take notice—if for no other reason than it has become a very expensive problem. Researchers estimate that between lost productivity, employee disengagement, turnover, and absenteeism, burnout costs employers as much as $190 billion a year.

Every year many new books and conference panels focus on employers' desires to create healthier workplace cultures. Recommendations run the gamut—from installing office nap pods and calming lighting to offering after-work yoga and paid volunteer days. I imagine soon employers will compete with each other to be the most "work-life balanced" in the same way they compete to be the most mission-driven. But independent of any particular policy, there are two preconditions for any organization that wants a healthy workplace culture: leaders must model the culture they hope to create, and companies must implement systems to protect employee time off.

I'm inspired by Mathilde Collin, CEO of the workplace communication platform Front, who is leading a movement of Silicon Valley leaders to talk openly about burnout and mental health. After going through Y Combinator's intensive startup accelerator program and building a multimillion-dollar company, Collin recognized that her tendency to overwork was not making her work—or her workplace—better.

Things came to a head in May 2017, when Collin was forced to step away from the company to tend to her mental health. Front's revenue and customer base were growing; the company had recently raised $10 million in funding. But although the business was healthy, Collin was not. She woke up one morning unable to look at her laptop without inducing a splitting headache. She got up to leave the house, but her legs wouldn't budge. "I have this deep anxiety that makes me hate life," she told her doctor at the time. After taking a few weeks off—one of her first breaks since starting Front almost four years prior—she decided to make some personal changes.

Collin removed all work-related apps from her phone, left

her laptop behind when she went on vacation, and started working from home on Thursday afternoons, with only a notebook and a pen. "As a leader, I know people will emulate my behavior," Collin wrote in a recent blog post. "After all, if 'the boss' can respond to email during their honeymoon vacation in the middle of the Sahara desert, who has a good excuse for not doing so?"

Collin's personal practices catalyzed progressive company-wide policies, such as frequent company-wide three-day weekends and monthly bonuses for employees who average less than two hours per day on their phones. But the bottom line is clear: unless company leaders model the culture they hope to create, it will never trickle down to the rest of the team.

Megan from chapter 4 had a similar realization during her break from the newsroom. While working at *Wired*, she never used to switch off the green dot that indicated her availability on Slack. She wanted reporters to feel like they could always reach her. She emphasized to her staff that her availability didn't necessarily mean that they had to always be available, too. But she later realized talk was not enough. "You can say sign off till you're blue in the face," she told me. "If people see that their bosses are on all the time, they'll feel some obligation to do the same."

I'm also inspired by the fully remote software startup Doist, which has a hundred employees in thirty-nine different countries. Rather than try to shoehorn everyone into a single calendar, Doist did away with company holidays altogether. Instead, the company offers employees forty days off a year to use as they see fit. Forty days off a year is a generous policy—especially for Americans whose average allotted time off is one-fourth as much—but the length is less impressive than the terms. Rather than place the burden on employees to negotiate their time off, Doist takes responsibility for protecting time off on their employees' behalf. Vacation time is compulsory.

Mandatory time off is the type of systemic change that precipitates a true change in culture. "Productivity and taking time off are yin and yang," Amir Salihefendić, Doist's founder and CEO, told me. "The ability to disengage, relax, and recharge is as important as being ambitious, organized, and productive."

## 3 • DEFINE YOUR VERSION OF "GOOD ENOUGH"

Toni Morrison held many titles in her lifetime: author, Nobel Prize winner, professor, jazz lover. In addition to writing, though, she always had a job. She worked on textbooks, taught English, and edited fiction. One of her first jobs was as a cleaning lady in her hometown of Lorain, Ohio.

One day, Morrison was complaining to her father about cleaning rich people's houses when her dad put down his coffee and said, "Listen. You don't live there. You live here. With your people. Go to work. Get your money. And come on home."

Morrison later wrote about the impact of her father's words in *The New Yorker*. "Since that conversation with my father I have never considered the level of labor to be the measure of myself," she recalled. "I have never placed the security of a job above the value of home."

Morrison's work was important, but it was her livelihood, not her life. When I think about what it means to have a good enough job, I think about Morrison's father's wisdom: Go to work. Get your money. Come on home.

The summer I spent power-washing other people's decks in high school taught me more than any of my classes the following semester. My first job in advertising taught me when to voice my opinion and when to shut up. Tech taught me pragmatism. Design taught me optimism. And journalism taught me to give a shit.

Through work, I've found meaning and purpose and lifelong friends. But the most important thing work has given me—the thing I need it to give to me—is enough money to live. At the end of the day, a job is an economic contract. It's an exchange of labor for money. The more clear-eyed we can be about that, the better.

Speaking about a job as a transaction may seem crass. We're told jobs are meant to be callings and vocations and passions, not mere paychecks. But companies already treat work transactionally. They hire employees who add value and fire employees who do not. Losing sight of this creates the conditions for exploitation.

I don't say this as a cynic. Rather, I think a more transactional approach to work liberates both employers and employees. It frees employers to focus on setting clear expectations for what good work looks like. It frees employees to advocate for fair compensation, rather than to assume that talking about money somehow undermines the company's best interest. Most importantly, it frees employees to treat work as a living and not as the entirety of their lives.

To be clear, I don't believe a more transactional approach to work needs to come at the expense of caring about your job or doing great work. There is nothing wrong with aligning your work with your interests or working hard to refine your craft. Rather, I'm advocating for a collective reorientation of our expectations. Much as it is unrealistic to expect a spouse to fulfill our every social, emotional, and intellectual need, it is unrealistic to expect a job to be our sole method of self-actualization. That's a burden our jobs are not designed to bear.

Kurt Vonnegut and Joseph Heller were once at a holiday party thrown by a billionaire hedge fund manager when Vonnegut asked Heller a question: "Joe, how does it make you feel to know that our host only yesterday may have made more money than your novel 'Catch-22' has earned in its entire history?"

"Well," Heller responded, "I've got something he can never have."

"What on earth could that be, Joe?" Vonnegut asked.

"The knowledge that I've got enough."

I love that story. Enough—or in this book's case "good enough"—is subjective. You choose what good enough means to you. Maybe it's a job for a certain company or a job that pays a certain wage. Maybe it's a job that has a certain title or a job that lets off at a certain hour. Whatever your good enough job is, recognize when you have it. Because then you can heed Morrison's father's advice: you can come on home.

After interviewing hundreds of people and spending many hours with the central characters of this book, I found that those with the healthiest relationships to their work had one thing in common: they all had a strong sense of who they were when they weren't working. That's what Divya found when she was forced to take a step back from Prameer, what Josh found after leaving the corporate world, and what Khe found in California.

To detach our sense of self-worth from our work, though, we must first develop a self that no boss or job title or market has the power to change. In Morrison's words, "You are not the work you do; you are the person you are." A good enough job is a job that allows you to be the person you want to be.

I began this book with a simple question: what do you do? I

want to end with a suggestion for how we might amend this canonical piece of American small talk. All it takes is adding two small words. "What do you *like to* do?" It's a question that allows you to define yourself on your own terms.

Maybe you like to read fiction. Maybe you like to cook Mediterranean food. Maybe you like to watercolor or to write. Maybe you do those things for work. Maybe you don't. Maybe that's good enough.

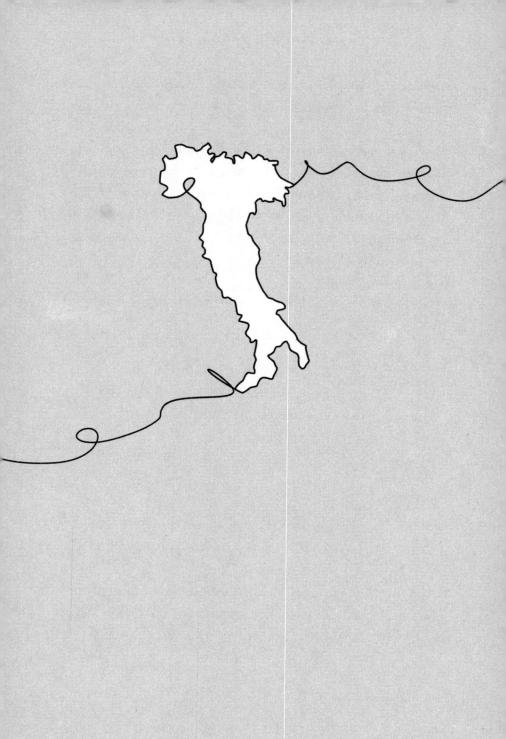

# Epilogue

It was three a.m. when my best friend called. I was twenty-four, and working at an ad agency in San Francisco. My friend Travis was living in Finland, which was nine hours ahead.

"Yo, sorry to wake you," he said.

"What's up, man?" I mumbled as I felt for a light switch to flick on.

"I don't know how I ended up here, but I'm on this travel blog and I came across this crazy flight deal leaving from San Francisco. I'm not sure how much longer it's going to last."

"What are you talking about?" I asked.

"There's this technical glitch on Priceline.com," he said. "If you enter a very specific itinerary from San Francisco to New

York, New York to Milan, and eight days later from Prague to Ho Chi Minh City, the whole ticket is $229. I'll send you the link."

The deal sounded too good to be true. But sure enough, when I clicked through, a blog post appeared with step-by-step instructions.

"Just bought my tickets!" someone wrote in the comments. "Since the flights are departing from the U.S., the chances are high that these fares will be honored," wrote someone else. An anonymous genius suggested that anyone who buys the mistake fare should wear a red hat for the first leg of the trip.

Sold. I bought the ticket that morning and promptly submitted my notice at work. A few weeks later, I arrived at San Francisco International Airport carrying a forty-five-liter backpack. As I walked through the terminal, I smiled at every red hat I passed.

In the year that followed, I called twenty-one countries home. I backpacked around Asia, and then made my way to Africa, where I traveled from Nairobi to Cape Town overland. From the road, I started to pitch articles to magazines and newspapers. I reported stories on the 2015 earthquake in Nepal, the changing tourism industry in Myanmar, and the opium trade in northern Thailand. While I'd previously written ads and marketing copy, it wasn't until I took time away from my default routine that I built the confidence to finally pursue journalism.

But the trip catalyzed more than just a career change for me. For the first time in my adulthood, I tasted a version of life that didn't feature work at the center. Some days I did little more than aimlessly wander the streets of a foreign city until dusk. During that trip was the first time I meditated, rode a motorbike, or wrote something without the expectation of sharing it with anyone else. I became acquainted with my nonproductive self.

Until I bought that plane ticket, you could have characterized my path in life as what former Yale English professor William Deresiewicz calls being a "world-class hoop jumper." In a now famous commencement speech, Deresiewicz observed how many of his students had been trained to achieve any goal set out for them. They could memorize any formula, ace any test, and "climb the greasy pole of whatever hierarchy they decide to attach themselves to." While ambitious and high achieving, they were "trapped in a bubble of privilege, heading meekly in the same direction." As one of Deresiewicz's students put it, Yale students were "excellent sheep."

I, too, was an excellent sheep. For the first twenty-four years of my life, my limited sense of purpose extended only to the next hoop set out for me. In middle school, I studied hard so I could be admitted to a selective high school. In high school, I chose extracurriculars that would make me an attractive candidate for a prestigious college. In college, I picked a major that would help me get a job, and I applied for internships in an industry, advertising, that I thought would impress my parents and peers.

My path, paved by the privilege of my upbringing—from San Francisco private school to Ivy League college to white-collar industry—could have been scripted. Instead, the three a.m. nudge from Travis and a Priceline glitch pushed me to ditch the script. I learned that I had more agency to determine work's role in my life than I thought.

Three weeks after turning in the manuscript of this book, I made another script-altering decision: I quit my job at the design firm where I had worked for the previous four years. After burning the candle at both ends to finish the book, I knew I needed a break. But as I hit send on my resignation email, I instantly felt a pang of doubt.

*Should I have stayed six more months to vie for my next promotion? What will my parents think? Am I irresponsible for quitting a stable job with nothing lined up on the other end?*

I recognized this doubt as common among workers I spoke to who had made similar choices to deprioritize work in their lives. It's easy to become enraptured by the performance review cycles, quarterly sales goals, and LinkedIn milestones laid out before us. One academic I interviewed (whose expertise is in "designing a more human-centered future of work") took only two weeks of maternity leave after giving birth to her first daughter because she couldn't imagine spending any more time away from her research. The pressure to work all the time runs deep—and it's reinforced by our government, our institutions, and our own minds.

It's easy to see a software engineer at Google or a Michelin-star chef or a Wall Street executive and think they've got it all figured out. But too often, we compare our insides to other people's outsides. If I've learned anything from talking to workers over the past few years, it's that even those who have all the résumé virtues are still negotiating the role that work plays in their lives.

To defy conventional expectations about work requires courage. Many elements of society—from the American healthcare system to the stigma around gaps in workers' résumés—make deprioritizing work unreasonably difficult. Not everyone is in a position to work fewer hours or to take a sabbatical and travel the world. But if you take away just one thing from this book, I hope it's this: on the other side of deprioritizing work is prioritizing life.

What we often lack—both as individuals and as a society—is the ability to imagine a less work-centric existence. So my question for you, dear reader, is: What's one small change you can make to elevate your nonwork self? Perhaps you schedule a weekly walk with your best friend. Maybe you get involved in a neighborhood group where no one has any idea how you make a living. Maybe you pick up a new hobby without the expectation of mastering it. What can you do to remind yourself that you exist on this earth to do more than produce economic value?

After I turned in the first draft of the book and quit my job, my fiancée and I bought tickets to spend a month with my family in southern Italy. We, unfortunately, paid the full airfare. The idea was to take time to reset after a period of intense work. I had been writing a book alongside a full-time job. She had been teaching fourth grade during a global pandemic.

But when we arrived in Italy, rest did not come easy for me. I quickly found myself tethered to my old habits. I checked my email first thing after I woke up in the morning. I stressed about how I would make money after the summer ended. I spent idle afternoons feeling as if I should be *doing* more.

But now, a few weeks into our time here, my body has adjusted to a new circadian rhythm. I credit the southern Italian sun, which quite literally forces me to slow down, and the indulgent lunches during which I linger at the table with cousins and aunts long after there is no more melon left to pick at. Slowly, I am relearning who I am without the constant doing.

Notably, work is not absent from my life here—I make time to write or edit most days—but it no longer feels like a fix for a restless leg. Work gives meaning to my life, but it is not the only source.

This morning I woke up late, spent some time working on this epilogue, ate lunch with my family, and took a nap with my partner. Tonight, we'll head into town for a drink. I'll look out for the fisherman.

# ACKNOWLEDGMENTS

First and foremost, thank you to the nine workers I profiled—
and to the many more with whom I spoke—for entrusting me
with your stories. Divya, Ryan, Fobazi, Megan, Taylor, Clarissa,
Josh, Brandon, and Khe, this book would not exist if not for you.

I never understood why authors referred to their books as
"projects" until I tried to complete one myself. Although there is
only one byline, writing a book is a team sport, and I feel blessed
to have a world-class team. My mentor Vauhini Vara was the
first person to tell me that I should write a book. Thank you for
elevating my ambition. There's no one whose opinion on writing I respect more. Thank you to Merry Sun, my whip-smart
editor, shepherd, and friend. I trust you deeply and am proud
of what we built together. And thank you to my agent Daniel
Greenberg for responding to a cold email from a first-time

author, and answering my inane questions about how the publishing industry works.

My life has been a series of lame excuses for why I'm not a real writer, so I appreciate everyone who has helped convince me otherwise. Thank you to Youth Speaks and the Excelano Project for helping me find my voice. Thank you to Lorene Cary for crossing out the first three pages of the first essay I wrote for you, and for telling me to "stop clearing my throat." Thank you to Janine Zacharia for telling me that I wasn't that good, and then helping me get better.

Thank you to Jennifer Maerz for giving me my first journalism assignment, and to Heather Landy, Matt Quinn, and Kevin Delaney for my first journalism job. Thank you to Mike Isaac for letting me look over your shoulder as you wrote your first book, and to Bill, Andrea, Shana, and everyone else at Lighthouse Writers Workshop for showing me that I could write one myself.

Thank you to the many thinkers, writers, and scholars whose ideas are woven throughout these pages. In particular, thank you to Derek Thompson, Sarah Jaffe, Alain de Button, Erin Cech, Ifeoma Ozoma, Jamie McCallum, Nikil Saval, C. Thi Nguyen, and Agnes Callard for shaping the way I think about work. A special thank-you to Anne Helen Petersen for your sharp notes and expert guidance. Your work is the foundation for much of this book and for how I think about a more just world.

Thank you to all the people who helped carry the book

across the finish line. Thank you to my colleagues at IDEO—and Deirdre Cerminaro, in particular—for giving me the space to work on this project alongside my full-time job. Thanks to my wonderful fact-checker, Emily Krieger, for having my back, and to my endnotes editor, Michael Burke, for your diligence. And thank you to the team at Portfolio, who have been such a pleasure to work with, including Veronica Velasco, Jen Heuer, Adrian Zackheim, and Kirstin Berndt.

This book would not have been possible without a small army of generous friends. In the first month of the pandemic, my friend Smiley Poswolsky introduced me to Rhaina Cohen, another aspiring author. Rhaina and I had "accountability chats" every Wednesday from April 2020 until each of us handed in our final manuscript. What a gift your friendship has been.

Thank you to Marty, Arielle, Paul, Kendall, Shoshana, Becca, Melissa, Jeff, John, Sabrina, and Lauren for reading shitty chapter drafts. Thank you to Ahmed, Rachel, Ian, Jean, Edgar, Lexi, Jonah, and Rose for offering me places to stay while I was working on the manuscript. Thank you to George, Fabian, Rachel, and Becky for helping me think through the cover. A special thanks to AJ Mapes for his eleventh-hour design therapy and help with the chapter illustrations.

Thank you to my homies—Joe, Travis, Sam, Anna, John, Peter, Pete, Rel, Katie, Ross, Isabel, and countless others—for the burritos and the belly laughs. Calling you my friends is the greatest joy of my life. To my siblings, Sam, Mary, Katie, Nina,

Sam, and Anna, thank you for moving through this world alongside me and counseling me through my semi-regular existential meltdowns. Thank you to my grandmothers, Mimi Feldman and Maria Conte, for always making me feel loved.

I'm blessed to have four parents, each of whom has given me a vital lens through which to see the world. Thank you to Teresa Pantaleo for sharing your love of reading, Gary Stolzoff for your love of listening, Suzi Alexander for your love of language, and Randall Kline for your love of the arts. Thank you for showing me what it means to live, and for always being my greatest cheerleaders.

And lastly, to my dear Katy. Thank you for holding space for me to write, for reading every draft, and for riding with me through the ups and downs along the way. Thank you for being my executive editor, my muse, and my partner. I feel so lucky to be navigating life with you. Te quiero mucho.

# NOTES

EPIGRAPH

ix **"He who knows he has enough"**: Lao Tsu Laozi, Jane English, and Gia-fu Feng, *Tao Te Ching*, trans. Gia-fu Feng and Jane English (New York: Vintage Books, 1972), 32.

INTRODUCTION

xii **a German short story:** Heinrich Böll and Leila Vennewitz, "Anecdote Concerning the Lowering of Productivity," *The Stories of Heinrich Boll* (Evanston, IL: Northwestern University Press, 1995), 628–30.

xiii **When analysts from Pew Research Center:** Patrick Van Kessel and Laura Silver, "Where Americans Find Meaning in Life Has Changed over the Past Four Years," Pew Research Center, November 18, 2021, https://www.pewresearch.org/fact-tank/2021/11/18/where-americans -find-meaning-in-life-has-changed-over-the-past-four-years.

xiii **gives their life meaning:** Travis Mitchell, "Where Americans Find Meaning in Life," Pew Research Center's Religion & Public Life Project, November 20, 2018, https://www.pewresearch.org/religion/2018/11/20/where-americans-find-meaning-in-life.

xiii **95 percent of American teenagers:** Juliana Menasce Horowitz and Nikki Graf, "Most U.S. Teens See Anxiety and Depression as a Major Problem Among Their Peers," Pew Research Center's Social & Demographic Trends Project, February 20, 2019, https://www.pewresearch.org/social-trends/2019/02/20/most-u-s-teens-see-anxiety-and-depression-as-a-major-problem-among-their-peers.

xiii **American work culture and management systems:** Robert Hauhart, "Exporting the American Dream: Global Implications," *International Journal of the Humanities*, no. 9 (2011): 1–11.

xiii **Journalist Derek Thompson dubbed:** Derek Thompson, "Workism Is Making Americans Miserable," *The Atlantic*, February 24, 2019, https://www.theatlantic.com/ideas/archive/2019/02/religion-workism-making-americans-miserable/583441.

xv **These pursuits are not always aligned:** The School of Life Library, *A Job to Love: A Practical Guide to Finding Fulfilling Work by Better Understanding Yourself* (London: The School of Life, 2018), 9.

xvi **But in the last half century:** Thompson, "Workism."

xvi **From Sweden to South Korea:** Laura Silver, Patrick van Kessel, Christine Huang, Laura Clancy, and Sneha Gubbala, "What Makes Life Meaningful? Views from 17 Advanced Economies," Pew Research Center's Global Attitudes Project, November 18, 2021, https://www

.pewresearch.org/global/2021/11/18/what-makes-life-meaningful
-views-from-17-advanced-economies.

xviii **In his 1930 essay:** John Maynard Keynes, "Economic Possibilities for
Our Grandchildren," in *Essays in Persuasion* (New York: W. W. Norton & Co., 1963), 358–73, http://www.econ.yale.edu/smith/econ116a
/keynes1.pdf.

xviii **As recently as 1965:** David Zahl, *Seculosity: How Career, Parenting,
Technology, Food, Politics, and Romance Became Our New Religion
and What to Do About It* (Minneapolis: Fortress Press, 2019), 87.

xix **In 1975, Americans and Germans:** Charlie Giattino, Esteban Ortiz-
Ospina, and Max Roser, "Working Hours," OurWorldinData.org,
2020, https://ourworldindata.org/working-hours.

xix **In 2021, Americans worked:** "Hours Worked," OECD Data, 2021,
https://data.oecd.org/emp/hours-worked.htm.

xix **In the 1950s, one in three:** Jill Lepore, "What's Wrong with the
Way We Work," *The New Yorker*, January 18, 2021, https://www
.newyorker.com/magazine/2021/01/18/whats-wrong-with-the-way
-we-work.

xix **There is a growing expectation:** Sarah Jaffe, *Work Won't Love You
Back: How Devotion to Our Jobs Keeps Us Exploited, Exhausted, and
Alone* (London: Hurst, 2021), 12.

xx **As sociologist Jamie K. McCallum writes:** Jamie K. McCallum,
*Worked Over: How Round-the-Clock Work Is Killing the American
Dream* (New York: Basic Books, 2020), 131.

xxi **Studies show that an "obsessive passion":** Robert J. Vallerand, Frederick L. Philippe, Julie Charest, and Yvan Paquet, "On the Role of Passion for Work in Burnout: A Process Model," *Journal of Personality* 78(1) (February 2010): 289–312.

xxi **Researchers have also found:** Lyman Stone, Laurie DeRose, and W. Bradford Wilcox, "How to Fix the Baby Bust," *Foreign Policy*, July 25, 2019, https://foreignpolicy.com/2019/07/25/how-to-fix-the -baby-bust.

xxi **record-high rates:** Jean M. Twenge, "Time Period and Birth Cohort Differences in Depressive Symptoms in the U.S., 1982–2013," *Social Indicators Research* 121(2) (April 2014).

xxi **Globally, more people die:** Christine Ro, "How Overwork Is Literally Killing Us," BBC Worklife, May 19, 2021, https://www .bbc.com/worklife/article/20210518-how-overwork-is-literally -killing-us.

xxiii **"What we do with this hour":** Annie Dillard, *The Writing Life* (New York: HarperCollins, 2009), 33.

xxiii **In the words of psychotherapist Esther Perel:** Esther Perel, "How Many of You Often Find Yourselves Bringing the Best of You to Work, and the Leftovers Home?," *Out in the Open*, CBC Radio, 2018, https://www.cbc.ca/player/play/1443267139554.

xxv **The stories that follow:** Studs Terkel, *Working: People Talk About What They Do All Day and How They Feel About What They Do* (New York: New Press, 2011), 1.

## CHAPTER 1: FOR WHAT IT'S WORTH

1 **"Sufficiency isn't two steps"**: Brené Brown, *The Gifts of Imperfection* (Center City, MN: Hazelden, 2010), 110.

10 **For example, in one study**: P. W. Linville, "Self-Complexity as a Cognitive Buffer Against Stress-Related Illness and Depression," *Journal of Personality and Social Psychology* 52(4) (April 1987): 663–76, https://pubmed.ncbi.nlm.nih.gov/3572732.

11 **"When you grow up an athlete"**: "Junior Seau's Death Ruled a Suicide," ESPN.com, May 3, 2012, https://www.espn.com/nfl/story/_/id/7888037/san-diego-county-medical-examiner-office-rules-junior-seau-death-suicide.

18 **And ironically, research shows**: Kevin J. Eschleman, Jamie Madsen, Gene Alarcon, and Alex Barelka, "Benefiting from Creative Activity: The Positive Relationships between Creative Activity, Recovery Experiences, and Performance-Related Outcomes," *Journal of Occupational and Organizational Psychology* 87(3) (September 2014): 579–98, https://bpspsychub.onlinelibrary.wiley.com/doi/abs/10.1111/joop.12064.

## CHAPTER 2: THE RELIGION OF WORKISM

21 **"There is no such thing"**: David Foster Wallace, "This Is Water," speech to Kenyon College graduating class, 2005, https://www.youtube.com/watch?v=PhhC_N6Bm_s.

22 **In 1990, only about 7 percent**: Ryan P. Burge, *The Nones: Where They*

*Came From, Who They Are, and Where They Are Going* (Minneapolis: Fortress Press, 2021), 82.

23 **Ryan's chart would go on:** Burge, *The Nones*, 2.

25 **"I felt like one of those factory workers":** Burge, *The Nones*, 134.

25 **The ancient Greeks saw work:** Hannah Arendt, *The Human Condition*, 2nd ed. (Chicago: University of Chicago Press, 1998), 82.

26 **The Latin word for business:** The School of Life, https://www.theschooloflife.com/article-themes/meaning.

26 **As the German sociologist Max Weber:** Max Weber, *The Protestant Ethic and the "Spirit" of Capitalism, and Other Writings* ([1905]; New York: Penguin Books, 2002).

27 **The prosperity gospel:** J. Matthew Wilson, ed., *From Pews to Polling Places: Faith and Politics in the American Religious Mosaic* (Washington, DC: Georgetown University Press, 2007), 141.

27 **According to Osteen:** Joel Osteen, "Have a Spirit of Excellence," *Joel Osteen Podcast*, November 17, 2020, https://www.happyscribe.com/public/joel-osteen-podcast/have-a-spirit-of-excellence-joel-osteen.

27 **In his bestselling book:** Joel Osteen, *Your Best Life Now: 7 Steps to Living at Your Full Potential* (New York, Boston, and Nashville: Faith Words [Kindle ed.], 2014), 21.

27 **Ryan has some theories:** Analysis of General Social Survey data by Ryan P. Burge, Eastern Illinois University, 2021.

29　**The Atheism subreddit:** https://www.reddit.com/r/atheism.

29　**The Christianity subreddit:** https://www.reddit.com/r/Christianity.

29　**Though the origin of the religious right:** Clyde Haberman, "Religion and Right-Wing Politics: How Evangelicals Reshaped Elections," *New York Times*, October 28, 2018, https://www.nytimes.com/2018/10/28/us/religion-politics-evangelicals.html.

30　**Scholars credit the Moral Majority:** Randall E. King, "When Worlds Collide: Politics, Religion, and Media at the 1970 East Tennessee Billy Graham Crusade," *Journal of Church and State*, March 22, 1997.

30　**In 1972, 55 percent:** Ryan Burge, Twitter, July 14, 2022, https://twitter.com/ryanburge/status/1547611343598981122?s=20&t=fyy7Dl_bcPRDx2HtXVLOaQ.

30　**In *Bowling Alone*:** Robert D. Putnam, *Bowling Alone: The Collapse and Revival of American Community* (New York: Simon & Schuster, 2000), 66.

31　**According to a study:** Will Tanner, Fjolla Krasniqi, and James Blagden, *Age of Alienation: The Collapse of Community and Belonging Among Young People, and How We Should Respond* (United Kingdom: Onward, 2021), https://www.ukonward.com/wp-content/uploads/2021/09/Age-of-Alienation-Onward.pdf.

31　**But as Derek Thompson writes:** Derek Thompson, "Workism Is Making Americans Miserable," *The Atlantic*, February 24, 2019, https://www.theatlantic.com/ideas/archive/2019/02/religion-workism-making-americans-miserable/583441.

34 **"The compelling reason":** Wallace, "This Is Water."

38 **In fact, workers with the same job title:** Amy Wrzesniewski, Nicholas LoBuglio, Jane Dutton, and Justin Berg, "Job Crafting and Cultivating Positive Meaning and Identity in Work," in *Advances in Positive Organizational Psychology*, ed. A. B. Bakker (Bingley, UK: Emerald Group Publishing Limited, 2013), 281–302.

38 **One common trait that researchers:** R. M. Ryan and E. L. Deci, "Self-Determination Theory and the Facilitation of Intrinsic Motivation, Social Development, and Well-Being," *American Psychologist* 55 (2000): 68–78.

## CHAPTER 3: THE LOVE OF LABOR

41 **"I have no dream job":** Casey Hamilton, "Work Is for Jerks," TikTok, https://www.tiktok.com/@mrhamilton/video/6847892192422382853.

41 **Over the course of that year:** Paul Vitello, "Richard Bolles Dies at 90; Wrote 'What Color Is Your Parachute?,'" New York Times, April 1, 2017, https://www.nytimes.com/2017/04/01/business/richard-bolles-dead-what-color-is-your-parachute.html.

42 *Parachute* **argued that work:** Richard N. Bolles, *What Color Is Your Parachute? 2020: A Practical Manual for Job-Hunters and Career-Changers* (California and New York: Ten Speed Press, 2019), 267.

42 **The initial print run:** Cal Newport, *So Good They Can't Ignore You: Why Skills Trump Passion in the Quest for Work You Love* (New York and Boston: Business Plus, 2012).

43 **In the fifty years:** Google Books Ngram Viewer, "dream job," https://
books.google.com/ngrams/graph?content=dream+job&year_start=1920
&year_end=2019&corpus=26&smoothing=3.

43 **"The problem with this gospel":** Derek Thompson, "Workism Is
Making Americans Miserable," *The Atlantic*, February 24, 2019, https://
www.theatlantic.com/ideas/archive/2019/02/religion-workism
-making-americans-miserable/583441.

45 **"You've got to find":** Steve Jobs, commencement address, Stanford
University, June 12, 2005, https://news.stanford.edu/2005/06/14/jobs
-061505.

45 **Artist Adam J. Kurtz:** Adam J. Kurtz, Work/Life Balance Print,
https://adamjk.com/products/do-what-you-love-print.

46 **Outside of class, she learned:** *The Library Quarterly: Information,
Community, Policy* 1(1) (Chicago: University of Chicago Press, January 2001): 1–27.

47 **The median pay for a librarian:** U.S. Bureau of Labor Statistics, Occupational Outlook Handbook, 2021, https://www.bls.gov/ooh/education
-training-and-library/librarians.htm.

47 **Four out of every five:** AFL-CIO Department for Professional Employees, "Library Professionals: Facts & Figures, 2021 Fact Sheet,"
https://www.dpeaflcio.org/factsheets/library-professionals-facts
-and-figures.

48 **that "meaningful work" even became:** Google Books Ngram Viewer,
"meaningful work," https://books.google.com/ngrams/graph?content

=meaningful+work&year_start=1800&year_end=2019&corpus =26&smoothing=3&direct_url=t1%3B%2Cmeaningful%20work %3B%2Cc0#; expansion of graph from Jamie K. McCallum, *Worked Over: How Round-the-Clock Work Is Killing the American Dream* (New York: Basic Books, 2020).

49  **These terms were further codified:** "Wage Chronology: Ford Motor Company, June 1941 to September 1973," *Bulletin of the United States Bureau of Labor Statistics*, No. 1787 (1973), https://fraser.stlouisfed .org/title/wage-chronology-ford-motor-company-june-1941 -september-1973-4882/wage-chronology-ford-motor-company-june -1941-september-1973-499659/fulltext.

49  **Since the 1970s, real wages:** Drew DeSilver, "For Most U.S. Workers, Real Wages Have Barely Budged in Decades," Pew Research Center, August 7, 2018, https://www.pewresearch.org/fact-tank /2018/08/07/for-most-us-workers-real-wages-have-barely-budged-for -decades.

49  **"With dollar-compensation no longer":** "America's Changing Work Ethic," CQ Researcher, December 14, 1979, https://library.cqpress .com/cqresearcher/document.php?id=cqresrre1979121400.

50  **Twenty years later:** Robin Kaiser-Schatzlein, "Why Your Boss Wants You to Love Your Job," *The Nation*, September 9, 2020, https:// www.thenation.com/article/culture/jamie-mccallum-worked-over -review.

50  **Today, nine out of ten people:** Shawn Achor, Andrew Reece, Gabriella Rosen Fischerman, and Alexi Robichaux, "9 Out of 10 People Are Willing to Earn Less Money to Do More-Meaningful Work,"

*Harvard Business Review*, November 6, 2018, https://hbr.org/2018/11 /9-out-of-10-people-are-willing-to-earn-less-money-to-do-more -meaningful-work.

50 **"It's become especially important"**: Sarah Jaffe, *Work Won't Love You Back: How Devotion to Our Jobs Keeps Us Exploited, Exhausted, and Alone* (London: Hurst, 2021), 2.

52 **"problem with vocational awe"**: Fobazi Ettarh, "Vocational Awe and Librarianship: The Lies We Tell Ourselves," *In the Library with the Lead Pipe*, January 10, 2018, https://www.inthelibrarywiththeleadpipe .org/2018/vocational-awe.

52 **The majority of zookeepers**: "Zookeeper Salary in the United States," Indeed, https://www.indeed.com/career/zookeeper/salaries.

53 **In a seminal study:** J. S. Bunderson and J. A. Thompson, "The Call of the Wild: Zookeepers, Callings, and the Double-Edged Sword of Deeply Meaningful Work," *Administrative Science Quarterly* 54(1) (2009): 32–57.

53 **"By cloaking the labor"**: Anne Helen Petersen, *Can't Even: How Millennials Became the Burnout Generation* (Boston and New York: Mariner Books, 2021), 68.

54 **By 2015, CEOs were paid:** Jill Lepore, "What's Wrong with the Way We Work," *New Yorker*, January 18, 2021, https://www.newyorker .com/magazine/2021/01/18/whats-wrong-with-the-way-we-work.

54 **"If you love what you do"**: Rachel Abrams, "On Wall Street, a Generation Gap on Work-Life Issues," *New York Times*, January 15, 2014,

https://archive.nytimes.com/dealbook.nytimes.com/2014/01/15/wall
-street-work-habits-show-generation-gap.

55 **Women made 83 cents:** "Median Earnings for Women in 2021 Were
83.1 Percent of the Median for Men," TED: The Economics Daily,
U.S. Bureau of Labor Statistics, January 24, 2022, https://www.bls.gov
/opub/ted/2022/median-earnings-for-women-in-2021
-were-83-1-percent-of-the-median-for-men.htm.

55 **Black women are typically paid:** Brandie Temple and Jasmine
Tucker, "Workplace Justice: Equal Pay for Black Women," National
Women's Law Center Fact Sheet, July 2017, https://nwlc.org/wp
-content/uploads/2017/07/Equal-Pay-for-Black-Women.pdf.

56 **As Petersen argues:** Petersen, *Can't Even*, 69.

57 **"I assure you Chicago Public Library staff":** Amy Dieg, Twitter, March
18, 2020, https://twitter.com/amydieg/status/1240410269970563072.

57 **The library where Fobazi worked:** Ashley Balcerzak, "NJ Coronavirus: Murphy Closes Nonessential Retail Businesses, Tells Residents
to Stay Home," NorthJersey.com, March 21, 2020, https://www.north
jersey.com/story/news/coronavirus/2020/03/21/coronavirus-nj
-shutdown-murphy-closes-nonessential-businesses/2884153001.

CHAPTER 4: LOSE YOURSELF

61 **"If I could go back in time":** "7 Questions 75 Artists 1 Very Bad
Year," *New York Times*, March 10, 2021, https://www.nytimes.com
/interactive/2021/03/10/arts/artists-coronavirus-lockdown.html.

63 **On Friday, December 10:** Matthew Yi, "Young Berkeley Journalists Broke Landlord Story Early," SFGate, January 21, 2000, https://www.sfgate.com/news/article/Young-Berkeley-journalists-broke-landlord-story-3270219.php.

63 *People* **magazine called her:** *Longform* podcast #302: Megan Greenwell, 1:06, https://longform.org/player/longform-podcast-302-megan-greenwell.

64 **"It feels really scary":** *Longform* podcast #302: Megan Greenwell.

64 **Megan and several other female leaders:** Laura Wagner, "This Is How Things Work Now at G/O Media," *Deadspin*, August 2, 2019, https://deadspin.com/this-is-how-things-work-now-at-g-o-media-1836908201.

64 **"The tragedy of digital media":** Megan Greenwell, "The Adults in the Room," *Deadspin*, August 23, 2019, https://deadspin.com/the-adults-in-the-room-1837487584.

67 **"This sense of identity":** Erik H. Erikson, *Childhood and Society* (New York: W. W. Norton and Company, 1993 [1950]), 42.

69 **Social scientist Arthur Brooks:** Arthur C. Brooks, "Why So Many People Are Unhappy in Retirement," *Atlantic*, May 7, 2020, https://www.theatlantic.com/family/archive/2020/05/what-the-heros-journey-teaches-about-happy-retirement/611194.

73 **Karl Marx theorized:** Karl Marx, "Estranged Labour," in *Economic and Philosophical Manuscripts of 1844*, https://www.marxists.org/archive/marx/works/1844/manuscripts/labour.htm.

73 **"We live in the most technologically connected age":** Vivek Murthy, "Work and the Loneliness Epidemic," *Harvard Business Review,* September 26, 2017, https://hbr.org/2017/09/work-and-the-loneliness-epidemic.

74 **Countless studies have proven:** Irina V. Popova-Nowak, "Work Identity and Work Engagement," working paper, George Washington University, 2010, https://www.ufhrd.co.uk/wordpress/wp-content/uploads/2010/08/9_5.pdf.

75 **"It's that community":** "Optimizing Space Itself with WeWork's Adam Neumann, Disrupt NY 2017," YouTube, https://www.youtube.com/watch?v=-EKOV71m-PY.

76 **Rabbi Abraham Joshua Heschel:** Abraham Joshua Heschel, *The Sabbath* (New York: FSG Classics, 2005), xiii.

79 **There's a saying in the Alcoholics Anonymous literature:** *Alcoholics Anonymous: The Story of How Many Thousands of Men and Women Have Recovered from Alcoholism*, 3rd rev. ed. (New York: Alcoholics Anonymous World Services, Inc., 1976).

## CHAPTER 5: WORKING RELATIONSHIPS

85 **"The only effective answer":** "Weekly Labor Quote—Thomas Donahue," NC State AFL-CIO, April 17, 2008, https://aflcionc.org/quote-donahue-thomas.

86 **The founders vowed never:** Stuart Dredge, "Kickstarter on Public Good over Private Riches: 'Don't Sell Out Your Values,'" *Guardian,*

November 3, 2015, https://www.theguardian.com/technology/2015
/nov/03/kickstarter-chooses-public-good-over-private-riches.

87 **Kickstarter pledged 5 percent:** Yancey Strickler, Perry Chen, and
Charles Adler, "Kickstarter Is Now a Benefit Corporation," *The
Kickstarter Blog*, September 21, 2015, https://www.kickstarter.com
/blog/kickstarter-is-now-a-benefit-corporation.

88 **"Our focus has always been":** ustwo cultural manifesto, https://
assets.ctfassets.net/gw5wr8vzz44g/55QKJCqQTuqgWc4ocuIYmC
/077ef0db4e38ca1965lae26264f041ea/ustwo-manifesto.pdf.

88 **Salesforce defines its corporate culture:** Jody Kohner, "The Real
Meaning Behind 'Salesforce Community,'" *The 360 Blog*, February
6, 2017, https://www.salesforce.com/blog/what-is-salesforce-ohana.

89 **One study from Gallup:** Tom Rath and Jim Harter, "Your Friends
and Your Social Well-Being," *Gallup Business Journal*, August 19,
2010, https://news.gallup.com/businessjournal/127043/friends-social
-wellbeing.aspx.

89 **Employees with friends at work:** Emma Seppälä and Marissa King,
"Having Work Friends Can Be Tricky but It's Worth It," *Harvard
Business Review*, August 8, 2017, https://hbr.org/2017/08/having-work
-friends-can-be-tricky-but-its-worth-it.

90 **A study from the workplace coaching startup BetterUp:** Gabriella
Rosen Kellerman and Andrew Reece, "The Value of Belonging at
Work: Investing in Workplace Inclusion," BetterUp, https://grow
.betterup.com/resources/the-value-of-belonging-at-work-the
-business-case-for-investing-in-workplace-inclusion-event.

91 **Similarly, friend-filled workplaces:** Julianna Pillemer, and Nancy P. Rothbard, "Friends without Benefits: Understanding the Dark Sides of Workplace Friendship," *The Academy of Management Review* 43(4) (February 2018).

91 **In one study:** Saera R. Khan and Lauren C. Howe, "Concern for the Transgressor's Consequences: An Explanation for Why Wrongdoing Remains Unreported," *Journal of Business Ethics* 173 (2021): 325–44.

92 **Sure, there was the occasional:** Davey Alba, "In the Beginning Was the Founder," *BuzzFeed News*, April 17, 2018, https://www.buzzfeed news.com/article/daveyalba/kickstarter-perry-chen-founder-worship -turmoil.

93 **The project in question:** *Always Punch Nazis*, Kickstarter, https:// www.kickstarter.com/projects/pilotstudios/always-punch-nazis.

93 **Then *Breitbart*, a right-wing news site:** Charlie Nash, "Kickstarter Ignores Terms of Service with 'Always Punch Nazis' Project," *Breitbart*, August 10, 2018, https://www.breitbart.com/tech/2018/08/10/kick starter-ignores-terms-of-service-with-always-punch-nazis-project.

95 **Though it was framed as a discussion:** "Kickstarter Union Oral History, Chapter 2: Catalyst," Engelberg Center, NYU Law, https:// eclive.engelberg.center/episodes/chapter-2-catalyst.

96 **"In that moment":** "Kickstarter Union Oral History, Chapter 2: Catalyst."

97 **At the height of organized labor:** "Union Members Summary," U.S.

Bureau of Labor Statistics Economic News Release, January 20, 2022, https://www.bls.gov/news.release/union2.nr0.htm.

98 **"There's a huge difference":** "Kickstarter Union Oral History, Chapter 3: Solidarity," Engelberg Center, NYU Law, https://eclive.engel berg.center/episodes/chapter-3-solidarity.

100 **"there's such a family culture":** Bryce Covert, "How Kickstarter Employees Formed a Union," *Wired*, May 27, 2020, https://www.wired .com/story/how-kickstarter-employees-formed-union.

102 **In an all-staff memo:** Bryan Menegus, "Leaked Memo Shows Kickstarter Senior Staffers Are Pushing Back Against Colleagues' Union Efforts," *Gizmodo*, March 21, 2019, https://gizmodo.com/leaked-memo -shows-kickstarter-senior-staffers-are-pushi-1833470597.

103 **In a company-wide email:** Bijan Stephen, "Kickstarter Will Not Voluntarily Recognize Its Employee Union," *The Verge*, May 15, 2019, https://www.theverge.com/2019/5/15/18627052/kickstarter-union-nlrb -election.

104 **"@kickstarter I will not be signing":** Clarissa Redwine, Twitter, September 12, 2019, https://twitter.com/clarissaredwine/status/117216725 1623124997.

108 **In June 2022:** OPEIU Webmaster, "Kickstarter United Wins Historic First Contract," Office & Professional Employees International Union (OPEIU), June 17, 2022, https://www.opeiu.org/Home/New sandMedia/TabId/2838/ArtMID/4815/ArticleID/2670/Kickstarter -United-Wins-Historic-First-Contract.aspx.

## CHAPTER 6: OFF THE CLOCK

111 **"My father built a time machine":** Charles Yu, *How to Live Safely in a Science Fictional Universe* (New York: Pantheon, 2010), 18.

112 **The word itself derives:** Alan W. Ewert and Jim Sibthorp, *Outdoor Adventure Education: Foundations, Theory, and Research* (Champaign, IL: Human Kinetics, 2014), 21.

112 **Athenians thought leisure:** Richard Kraus, *Recreation & Leisure in Modern Society* (United States: Jones and Bartlett, 1998), 38.

112 **Aristotle believed leisure:** Gene Bammel and Lei Lane Burrus-Bammel, *Leisure and Human Behavior* (Dubuque, IA: William C. Brown, 1992).

113 **the average American works:** "Hours Worked," OECD Data (2021), https://data.oecd.org/emp/hours-worked.htm.

113 **In the 1970s, the average worker:** Charlie Giattino, Esteban Ortiz-Ospina, and Max Roser, "Working Hours," revised 2020, Our World in Data, https://ourworldindata.org/working-hours.

113 **But in the last fifty years:** Derek Thompson, "The Free-Time Paradox in America," *The Atlantic*, September 13, 2016, https://www.theatlantic.com/business/archive/2016/09/the-free-time-paradox-in-america/499826.

115 **The gig platform Fiverr:** Ellen Scott, "People Are Not Pleased with Fiverr's Deeply Depressing Advert," *Metro 50*, March 10, 2017, https://

metro.co.uk/2017/03/10/people-are-not-pleased-with-fiverrs-deeply
-depressing-advert-6500359.

116 **the lowest-earning quintile:** Valerie Wilson and Janelle Jones, "Working Harder or Finding It Harder to Work," Economic Policy Institute, February 22, 2018, https://www.epi.org/publication/trends-in
-work-hours-and-labor-market-disconnection.

116 **Even in countries like Norway and Germany:** "Gig Economy 2021," PwC Legal, 2021, https://www.pwclegal.be/en/FY21/gig-economy
-report-v3-2021.pdf.

117 **The medical residency model:** James R. Wright, Jr., and Norman S. Schachar, "Necessity Is the Mother of Invention: William Stewart Halsted's Addiction and Its Influence on the Development of Residency Training in North America," *Canadian Journal of Surgery* 63(1) (February 2020): E13–18, https://www.ncbi.nlm.nih.gov/pmc
/articles/PMC7828946.

120 **But there were a few problems:** Jill Lepore, "Not So Fast: Scientific Management Started as a Way to Work. How Did It Become a Way of Life?," *New Yorker*, October 12, 2009, https://www.newyorker.com
/magazine/2009/10/12/not-so-fast.

120 **He described the average steelworker:** Bruno Dubuc, "The Organization of Manual Labour," *The Brain from Top to Bottom*, n.d., https://
thebrain.mcgill.ca/flash/i/i_06/i_06_s/i_06_s_mou/i_06_s_mou.html.

121 **At UnitedHealth Group:** Jodi Kantor and Arya Sundaram, "The Rise of the Worker Productivity Score," *New York Times*, August 14,

2022, https://www.nytimes.com/interactive/2022/08/14/business/worker -productivity-tracking.html.

121 **Eight of the ten largest:** Kantor and Sundaram, "The Rise of the Worker Productivity Score."

128 **Brain scans show that idle time:** Rebecca J. Compton, Dylan Gear- inger, and Hannah Wild, "The Wandering Mind Oscillates: EEG Alpha Power Is Enhanced during Moments of Mind-Wandering," *Cognitive, Affective, & Behavioral Neuroscience* 19 (2019): 1184–91, https://link.springer.com/article/10.3758/s13415-019-00745-9.

128 **In one study, four days:** Ruth Ann Atchley, David L. Strayer, and Paul Atchley, "Creativity in the Wild: Improving Creative Reason- ing Through Immersion in Natural Settings," *PLoS One* 7(12) (2012): e51474, https://journals.plos.org/plosone/article?id=10.1371/journal.pone .0051474.

130 **"Young people feel a kind of pressure":** Elsie Chen, "These Chinese Millennials Are 'Chilling,' and Beijing Isn't Happy," *New York Times,* July 3, 2021, https://www.nytimes.com/2021/07/03/world/asia /china-slackers-tangping.html.

131 **A 2014 study of munition workers:** John Pencavel, "The Productiv- ity of Working Hours," *The Economic Journal* 125, no. 589 (2015): 2052–76, http://www.jstor.org/stable/24738007.

132 **"Worn down by long hours":** Gudmundur D. Haraldsson and Jack Kellam, "Going Public: Iceland's Journey to a Shorter Working Week," Autonomy, July 4, 2021, https://autonomy.work/portfolio/ice landsww.

133 **"This [reduction in hours] shows":** Haraldsson and Kellam, "Going Public."


CHAPTER 7: WORK HARD, GO HOME

137 **"The caveman was undoubtedly very pleased":** Rob Harris, *London's Global Office Economy: From Clerical Factory to Digital Hub* (United Kingdom: CRC Press, 2021), 278.

139 **"Orwell warns that we will be overcome":** Neil Postman, *Amusing Ourselves to Death: Public Discourse in the Age of Show Business* (New York: Penguin Books, 2005), xix.

140 **In the courtyard sat the workers:** Nikil Saval, *Cubed: The Secret History of the Workplace* (New York: Anchor Books, 2014), 68.

141 **"With no time to shop for groceries":** Karen Ho, *Liquidated: An Ethnography of Wall Street* (Durham, NC: Duke University Press, 2009), 90.

142 **"The modern knowledge worker":** Cal Newport, *A World without Email: Reimagining Work in an Age of Communication Overload* (New York: Portfolio, 2021), 12.

146 **For one of Rothbard's studies:** "Integrators and Segmentors: Managing Remote Workers," Knowledge at Wharton, August 31, 2020, https://knowledge.wharton.upenn.edu/article/integrators-segmentors-managing-remote-workers.

147 **On the other end of the spectrum:** Adam Grant, "When Work Takes Over Your Life," *WorkLife with Adam Grant*, TED podcast, https://

www.ted.com/talks/worklife_with_adam_grant_when_work_takes
_over_your_life.

148 **During Brandon's early years:** "The Art of Not Buying Things," *Thoughts from Inside the Box,* July 9, 2016, https://frominsidethebox .com/post/the-art-of-not-buying-things/5718532058775552.

148 **"It wasn't that my workload":** "Striking a Balance," *Thoughts from Inside the Box,* October 3, 2015, https://frominsidethebox.com/view ?key=5768755258851328.

150 **One study of over 3 million workers:** Evan DeFilippis, Stephen Michael Impink, Madison Singell, Jeffrey T. Polzer, and Raffaella Sadun, "Collaborating during Coronavirus: The Impact of COVID-19 on the Nature of Work," National Bureau of Economic Research, Working Paper 27612, July 2020, https://www.nber.org/system/files /working_papers/w27612/w27612.pdf.

152 **Executives love to tout:** Claire Cain Miller, "Do Chance Meetings at the Office Boost Innovation? There's No Evidence of It," *New York Times,* June 23, 2021, https://www.nytimes.com/2021/06/23/upshot /remote-work-innovation-office.html.

152 **In fact, studies show that productivity:** Ethan S. Bernstein and Stephen Turban, "The Impact of the 'Open' Workspace on Human Collaboration," *Philosophical Transactions of the Royal Society B,* July 2, 2018, https://royalsocietypublishing.org/doi/10.1098/rstb.2017.0239.

152 **The open office:** Anne Helen Petersen, *Can't Even: How Millennials Became the Burnout Generation* (New York: Houghton Mifflin Harcourt, 2020), 129.

153 **We drove south down:** "A Fighter Jet and Friends in Congress: How Google Got Access to a NASA Airfield," Tech Transparency Project, September 9, 2020, https://www.techtransparencyproject.org/articles /fighter-jet-and-friends-congress-how-google-got-access-nasa -airfield.

## CHAPTER 8: THE STATUS GAME

157 **"When you get to my age":** Warren Buffett, Terry Leadership Speaker Series, Terry College of Business at the University of Georgia, July 18, 2001, YouTube, https://www.youtube.com/watch?v=2a9Lx9J8uSs.

162 **Instead, 92 percent agreed:** "Success Index," Populace/Gallup, 2019, https://static1.squarespace.com/static/59153bc0e6f2e109b2a85cbc/t/5d 939cc86670c5214abe4b50/1569955251457/Populace+Success+Index.pdf.

163 **Americans are largely driven:** David Brooks, "The Moral Bucket List," *New York Times*, April 11, 2015, https://www.nytimes.com/2015 /04/12/opinion/sunday/david-brooks-the-moral-bucket-list.html.

163 **People with high status:** Paola Zaninotto, et al., "Socioeconomic Inequalities in Disability-free Life Expectancy in Older People from England and the United States: A Cross-national Population-Based Study," *The Journals of Gerontology, Series A* 75(5) (May 2020): 906–13, https://academic.oup.com/biomedgerontology/article/75/5/906 /5698372.

163 **As Loretta Graziano Breuning writes:** Loretta Graziano Breuning, *Status Games: Why We Play and How to Stop* (Lanham, MD: Rowman & Littlefield, 2021), ix.

165 **Video games offer:** C. Thi Nguyen, "Gamification and Value Capture," chap. 9 of *Games: Agency as Art* (New York: Oxford Academic, 2020), online ed., https://doi.org/10.1093/oso/9780190052089 .003.0009.

166 **In a fourteen-year study:** Wendy Nelson Espeland and Michael Sauder, *Engines of Anxiety: Academic Rankings, Reputation, and Accountability* (New York: Russell Sage Foundation, 2016).

169 **The ensuing paper:** Mark R. Lepper, David Greene, and Richard E. Nisbett, "Undermining Children's Intrinsic Interest with Extrinsic Reward: A Test of the 'Overjustification' Hypothesis," *Journal of Personality and Social Psychology* 28(1) (1973): 129–37, https://psycnet.apa .org/record/1974-10497-001.

169 **As Daniel Pink wrote:** Daniel H. Pink, *Drive: The Surprising Truth about What Motivates Us* (New York: Riverhead Books, 2011), 36.

170 **Regardless of whether people had:** Grant Edward Donnelly, Tianyi Zheng, Emily Haisley, and Michael I. Norton, "The Amount and Source of Millionaires' Wealth (Moderately) Predicts Their Happiness," *Personality and Social Psychology Bulletin* 44(5) (May 2018): 684–99, https://www.hbs.edu/faculty/Pages/item.aspx?num=53540.

170 **Steve Nash, an adviser:** Zach Lowe, "Why the Collapse of the Warriors Feels So Abrupt," ESPN.com, July 2, 2019, https://www .espn.com/nba/story/_/id/27100698/why-collapse-warriors-feels -abrupt.

170 **Michael Phelps, the most decorated Olympian:** Karen Crouse, "Seeking Answers, Michael Phelps Finds Himself," *New York Times*, June

24, 2016, https://www.nytimes.com/2016/06/26/sports/olympics/michael
-phelps-swimming-rehab.html.

173 **Games tell us exactly:** Nguyen, "Gamification and Value Capture."

174 **Today the newsletter has more:** "Supercharge Your Productivity,"
*RadReads*, https://radreads.co/courses.


CHAPTER 9: A WORLD WITH LESS WORK

179 **"People tend to personalize":** "We Are All Burnt Out," *The Cut Podcast*, September 1, 2021, https://www.thecut.com/2021/09/the-cut-pod
cast-we-are-all-burned-out.html.

181 **In the words of author James Clear:** James Clear, *Atomic Habits:
Tiny Changes, Remarkable Results: An Easy & Proven Way to Build
Good Habits & Break Bad Ones* (New York: Avery, 2018), 33.

182 **"When cultivating a healthy working culture":** Anne Helen Petersen, "Just Because Your Early Career Was Hell Doesn't Mean
Others' Has to Be," *Culture Study*, June 1, 2021, https://annehelen
.substack.com/p/just-because-your-early-career-was.

183 **"Let's not delude ourselves":** Luc Pansu, "Evaluation of 'Right to
Disconnect' Legislation and Its Impact on Employee's Productivity,"
*International Journal of Management and Applied Research* 5(3) (2018):
99–119, https://www.ijmar.org/v5n3/18-008.html.

183 **In 2017, a paltry:** "Japan Offers Most Paid Leave for Fathers in
World, but Few Take It," *Kyodo News*, June 13, 2019, https://english

.kyodonews.net/news/2019/06/78563c3875f3-japan-offers-most-paid
-leave-for-fathers-in-world-but-few-take-it.html.

184 **The activist Dana White:** Dana White, Twitter status, September 6,
2020, https://twitter.com/itsdanawhite/status/1302708081437089792.

186 **It could mean forgiving the anvil:** Anna Helhoski, "How Many
Americans Have Student Loan Debt?," NerdWallet, May 20, 2021,
https://www.nerdwallet.com/article/loans/student-loans/how-many
-americans-have-student-loan-debt.

186 **It could mean expanding:** Chuck Marr, Chye-Ching Huang, Arloc
Sherman, and Brandon Debot, "EITC and Child Tax Credit Promote Work, Reduce Poverty, and Support Children's Development,
Research Finds," Center on Budget and Policy Priorities, October 1,
2015, https://www.cbpp.org/research/federal-tax/eitc-and-child-tax
-credit-promote-work-reduce-poverty-and-support-childrens.

186 **Or it could mean reimagining:** Emma Wager, Jared Ortaliza, and
Cynthia Cox, "How Does Health Spending in the U.S. Compare to
Other Countries?," Peterson-KFF Health System Tracker, January
21, 2022, https://www.healthsystemtracker.org/chart-collection/health
-spending-u-s-compare-countries-2.

187 **As a reference point:** https://www.stocktondemonstration.org.

187 **The stipend also afforded Zohna:** "Participant Story: Zohna," https://
www.stocktondemonstration.org/participant-stories/zohna.

188 **But perhaps the most encouraging finding:** https://www.stockton
demonstration.org.

NOTES

188 **A Pew Research survey found:** Kim Parker and Juliana Menasce Horowitz, "Majority of Workers Who Quit a Job in 2021 Cite Low Pay, No Opportunities for Advancement, Feeling Disrespected," Pew Research Center, March 9, 2022, https://www.pewresearch.org/fact-tank/2022/03/09/majority-of-workers-who-quit-a-job-in-2021-cite-low-pay-no-opportunities-for-advancement-feeling-disrespected.

188 **But the majority of the nearly 50 million:** Lucia Mutikani, "U.S. Labor Market Very Tight, Job Openings Near Record High in January," Reuters, March 9, 2022, https://www.reuters.com/world/us/us-job-openings-slip-january-still-close-record-highs-2022-03-09.

190 **But as *The Wall Street Journal* noted:** Andrea Petersen, "Metaphor of Corporate Display: 'You Work, and Then You Die,'" *Wall Street Journal*, November 8, 1996, https://www.wsj.com/articles/SB847408435479148500.

190 **A 2021 survey from:** "SHRM Survey: Nearly Half of U.S. Workers Feel Mentally, Physically Exhausted by End of Workday," press release, SHRM, May 4, 2021, https://www.shrm.org/about-shrm/press-room/press-releases/pages/nearly-half-of-us-workers-feel-mentally-physically-exhausted-by-end-of-workday.aspx.

190 **Only 36 percent of employees:** Jim Harter, "U.S. Employee Engagement Data Hold Steady in First Half of 2021," Gallup Workplace, July 29, 2021, https://www.gallup.com/workplace/352949/employee-engagement-holds-steady-first-half-2021.aspx.

190 **Another study, this one from McKinsey:** Aaron De Smet, Bonnie Dowling, Bryan Hancock, and Bill Schaninger, "The Great Attrition Is Making Hiring Harder. Are You Searching the Right Talent Pools?,"

237

*McKinsey Quarterly*, July 13, 2022, https://www.mckinsey.com/business
-functions/people-and-organizational-performance/our-insights/the
-great-attrition-is-making-hiring-harder-are-you-searching-the-right
-talent-pools.

190 **Notably, 47.8 million Americans actually did quit:** Mutikani,
"U.S. Labor Market Very Tight, Job Openings Near Record High in
January."

190 **Researchers estimate that between lost productivity:** Eric Garton,
"Employee Burnout Is a Problem with the Company, Not the Person," *Harvard Business Review*, April 6, 2017, https://hbr.org/2017
/04/employee-burnout-is-a-problem-with-the-company-not-the
-person.

191 **"I have this deep anxiety":** Cameron Albert-Deitch, "Hard Lessons
and Simple Routines Helped These Founders Beat the Stress of
2020," *Inc.*, November 2020, https://www.inc.com/magazine/202011
/cameron-albert-deitch/front-mathilde-collin-laurent-perrin-cancer
-depression-crisis.html.

192 **"As a leader":** Mathilde Collin, "How I Took a Week Off Work
and Completely Disconnected," *Front Page*, May 6, 2022, https://
front.com/blog/how-i-took-a-week-off-work-and-completely
-disconnected.

193 **offers employees forty days off a year:** Chris Kolmar, "50+ Telling
Paid Time Off (PTO) Statistics [2022]: Average PTO in the United
States," Zippia, August 18, 2022, https://www.zippia.com/advice/pto
-statistics/#:~:text=After%20extensive%20research%2C%20our
%20data,days%20of%20PTO%20in%202018.

194 **"Since that conversation":** Toni Morrison, "The Work You Do, the Person You Are," *New Yorker*, May 29, 2017, https://www.newyorker .com/magazine/2017/06/05/the-work-you-do-the-person-you-are.

195 **"Joe, how does it make you feel":** Kurt Vonnegut, Jr., "Joe Heller" (poem), *New Yorker*, May 16, 2005.

196 **"You are not the work":** Morrison, "The Work You Do, the Person You Are."

EPILOGUE

201 **In a now famous commencement speech:** William Deresiewicz, "Solitude and Leadership," *The American Scholar*, March 1, 2010, https:// theamericanscholar.org/solitude-and-leadership.

201 **While ambitious and high achieving:** William Deresiewicz, *Excellent Sheep: The Miseducation of the American Elite and the Way to a Meaningful Life* (New York: Free Press, 2014), 3.